The stories of creation, Ada.
to most of us, but Jane Rubietta's beautifully written devotional offers a spiritual depth and richness that's life-giving. Even more, she shows the relevance of each Scripture to our busy, everyday lives. Each page overflows with the matchless love of God, filling a deep well of joy in readers' hearts. I highly recommend this book as part of anyone's daily quiet time.

—LYNN AUSTIN, author of The Restoration Chronicles series

Finding Your Way is deep, wise, and surprisingly original. Jane Rubietta discovers fresh insights for veteran readers and those new to devotionals for beginning their days in God's Word. She bravely reveals personal vulnerabilities and wisely uses everyday language for those of us who can best discover holiness in her straightforward, yet exquisite detail. Her rich descriptions and engaging anecdotes make *Finding Your Way* come alive.

—CAROLYN CURTIS, author of *Women and C.S. Lewis*

Reading *Finding Your Way* by Jane Rubietta will help you dig a little deeper into Genesis, stand in more awe of the Creator, look more honestly at the person you see in the mirror, and move closer to the God who formed you.

—PAM FARREL, author of *7 Simple Skills for Every Woman*

I hadn't read too many pages before I had "ah-ha" and "I never thought of that" moments. Not only is this book great for personal use, but I see great possibilities with small groups as well. Reading, discussing, and sharing new insights make the potential for growth so exciting.

—LINDA G. HARDIN, women's ministries consultant, Church of the Nazarene

These are transformational devotionals with great depth. Jane offers a fresh and compelling vision of the lives of Adam, Eve, and Noah, but more than rich words, she has coupled biblical truth with practical ways in which to personally walk from pain to purpose. Especially transformational can be her guide, which leads one to read, contemplate, and act. There is rich and practical depth in these pages.

—JO ANNE LYON, General Superintendent of The Wesleyan Church

Each day we are treated to deftly woven stories and fascinating teaching from the beginning of the beginning—creation, Adam and Eve, Noah, and all the vastness included in those early days. I realized with delight that this was the first time I had spent time each day in that fascinating and foundational book of Genesis. My favorite part was the "Traveling Mercy" benediction, sending me on my own journey forward, to live what I had learned.

—LUCINDA SECREST MCDOWELL, author of *Live These Words*

Jane Rubietta invites us on a journey from pain to purpose through the lives of Adam and Eve and Noah that will surprise and inspire you. Packed with Scripture and written with personal witness and wisdom, this ninety-one-day adventure calls us to not only understand, but also live in the promise of full, new life.

—ANDREA SUMMERS, director of women's ministry for The Wesleyan Church

FINDING YOUR WAY

FROM PAIN TO PURPOSE—
THE LIVES OF ADAM AND NOAH

Jane Rubietta

wesleyan
PUBLISHING HOUSE
wphstore.com

Copyright © 2015 by Jane Rubietta
Published by Wesleyan Publishing House
Indianapolis, Indiana 46250
Printed in the United States of America
ISBN: 978-0-89827-894-1
ISBN (e-book): 978-0-89827-895-8

Library of Congress Cataloging-in-Publication Data

Rubietta, Jane.
  Finding your way : from pain to purpose, the lives of Adam and Noah / Jane
Rubietta.
     pages cm
  ISBN 978-0-89827-894-1 (pbk.)
  1. Bible. Genesis, I-XI--Meditations. 2. Adam (Biblical figure)--Meditations
3. Eve (Biblical figure)--Meditations. 4. Devotional calendars. I. Title.
  BS1235.54.R833 2015
  242'.5--dc23

                          2015013594

All Scripture quotations, unless otherwise indicated, are taken from the Holy
Bible, New International Version®, NIV ®. Copyright © 1973, 1978, 1984, 2011
by Biblica, Inc. Used by permission of Zondervan. All rights reserved worldwide
www.zondervan.com. The "NIV" and "New International Version" are trademarks
registered in the United States Patent and Trademark Office by Biblica, Inc.

Scripture quotations marked (AMP) are taken from the Amplified Bible, Copyright
© 1954, 1958, 1962, 1964, 1965, 1987 by The Lockman Foundation. Used by
permission.

Scripture quotations marked (NASB) are taken from the *New American Standard
Bible®*, Copyright © 1960, 1962, 1963, 1968, 1971, 1972, 1973, 1975, 1977
1995 by The Lockman Foundation. Used by permission.

Scripture quotations marked (MSG) are taken from *The Message*. Copyright ©
1993, 1994, 1995, 1996, 2000, 2001, 2002. Used by permission of NavPress
Publishing Group.

Scripture quotations marked (NET) are from the NET Bible® copyright ©1996–2006
by Biblical Studies Press, L.L.C. http://bible.org. All rights reserved. Used by
permission.

Cover photo: Cody Rayn

For Abigail Kathryn, who asks, "Papa, can you tell us about Genesis?" May you always want to know and love the Word of God and the God who keeps his Word and the Word made flesh who came to earth to love you, sweet one.

CONTENTS

For free shepherding resources, visit
www.wphresources.com/findingyourway.

INTRODUCTION

In all the lost seasons of my life, the book of Genesis grounds me. It lays down a path, a means of finding my way back to God, back to reality, back to what really matters in this world. Back to the certainty that God created, God loves, and God guides.

Finding Your Way: From Pain to Purpose—the Lives of Adam and Noah is a conversion handbook, introducing an amazing alchemy where the elements of our lives—the pain, the problems, the people-dysfunction—convert into passion and purpose, and become more than the sum of their parts. We follow Adam and Eve and their descendants and recognize God in the story, as God converts the pain and redirects the first generations of humanity, and us, through detours and diversions.

Finding Your Way is also a handbook on creativity—God's, yours, and the world's. It is for leaders, laypeople, artists, and intellectuals. For the questioner, the doubter, the faithful, and all of us who hope that life is bigger than the problems we face. Larger than just getting by, covering the bills, and smiling at the right times with the right rhetoric. It is; I promise. More importantly than that, God promises.

Our "In the beginning" book, Genesis, reminds us that, through pain, through problems, and through the mudslides of disappointment and the mountain climbs of rocky discouragement, the path will lead us home. En route, what a bonus to discover that the pain encountered actually becomes critical to finding our passion. And our purpose.

To begin this season of deeper devotion in Genesis, read chapters 1–11 in one sitting, to see the sweep and flow of the story of beginnings. A journal, a daily record as you process your journey with God and find your way, may help you remember God's nudges and challenges, the words of conviction, and the spots of quickening.

A Scripture opens each day's reading. Read the verse's context. Wait with those words. One surprising element of an approach to Scripture that includes deeper reading and devotion is how many facts, ironies, connections, and ah-ha's appear.

Each reading closes with a Traveling Mercy, a benediction God might speak over you, your day, and your life as you find your way. We hear blessings over us too seldom. Read this aloud, externalizing the words, so you hear them as though God speaks them over you.

The Note to Self is the brief reminder we carry through our day, inviting us to take deliberate action on the words we've read, whether repurposing or purposing for the first time. Challenge yourself to work through that note.

This is just one miracle of the Scriptures, how they pulse with life, how one day a new word you never noticed appears and God knocks you back from your boredom with your so-called but not-very quiet time. Sometimes with just the slightest twist, tears sting as the Holy Spirit leans close so you almost feel God's breath. Words light up like a neon sign or a night light or a match flaring in the dark. Suddenly we recognize God's incredible plan, God's amazing Word, the truth found in those words, and how much God loves us.

That, perhaps, is my single largest takeaway as I've loved and pored over God's Word, dissected verses and paragraphs and chapters, looked at words in the original languages, studied storylines, and gleaned new insights: God is crazy about us and has gone to incredible lengths to prove it to us. Though our paths are winding—and I don't know anyone who found their way to be a long straight line on smooth level ground, nor do I know anyone who felt particularly well-equipped with the best hiking shoes, with expert trail knowledge, or with an endless supply of trail mix—God is the helicopter in the sky overhead, always with the light beaming down to find, lead, and direct us. God is also the companion on the trail with us.

Thanks for joining the excursion as we find our way. We will, I promise, find the God who makes a way, and find God faithful along the way. We will find our way together, ultimately living a life of deeper devotion—a life that makes a difference. We fulfill our purpose using the only means available to us: life, lived daily.

Welcome to Genesis, to the beginning. Welcome to real life. Welcome to the arms of the One who loves you more than life itself.

DECEMBER DEVOTIONS

DECEMBER 1

INEXPRESSIBLE

In the beginning God created the heavens and the earth.
Now the earth was formless and empty, darkness was over the surface
of the deep, and the Spirit of God was hovering over the waters.

—Genesis 1:1–2

Genesis. The book of beginnings. The earth's. Yours. Mine. These few pages have captured the imagination and hearts of poets, artists, theologians, and scientists for centuries. Fingers itch to pen words of response. To seize paint and brush, and to prepare a canvas. To feel the ancient sculpting dirt, and to live that first scoop of creation. To dance over the lines and stories. Our minds whir, unable to comprehend or communicate the brilliance of the "In the beginning" of our world and lives.

"In the beginning." The three words, perhaps the best-known words of all time, have captivated us, awakening longing for expression, a desire to know God's glory and the God of such glory. The best words ever written about this beginning of the world and of us are simple, spare, and succinct. Yet they are also full-bodied, burgeoning with the unsaid.

How are we to reinterpret the glory, the power, of an indescribable start? Explain it; explain it away. To try to depict it is almost to minimalize it.

I will, as will you, of course, still try to put into words the wordless, to express the inexpressible, to allow fingers to dance over the keys, eyes closed, experiencing.

Imagine Adam and Eve telling the story. They, the first witnesses on the scene. Creation, redolent with new-world scent. The mystery, retold with deep sparkling eyes and hushed tones. The grandeur, painted with words and gestures. It is a whole body tale, demanding a full range of interpretation. We join in with circling arms, jazz hands, tiptoes, and dancing feet.

Of all the arts, perhaps music is the one medium that might capture the layers and richness of the genesis, the world's genesis, our personal genesis, the experiential qualities of the greatest mystery of all time. The great wonder beneath and around and exceeding all the wonders of the world. Any other attempt at visualizing falls short, impossibly inadequate to encompass miracle. When words mute, however, music swells into expression.

Hear the deep, brooding undertones, the husky bass strings vibrating, the slow tumble of mallets on timpani. The expectancy in those sounds, the drawing out, the releasing of all that is. But gradually, so smoothly and simply that we are measures into the creation before we realize that the adventure has already swept us away, out of our time-bound, fact-based existence into a universe untethered and untried. All for us.

Explore! Listen! Wonder upon wonder. Crescendoing wonder—fuller, bigger, the sounds pealing across the expanse of universe, the untried sky, the unseen night, and the veil-covered day. The brooding chaos, the breath of God hovering above. And then, the separation. Light emerging from dark.

The formless, the void, shapeless chaos and brooding potential. The story for all of us at some point in our existence. In our vast unknowns and wordless fears, this one story anchors you and me in place, in time, and in a relationship with the always-present but then-unseen God. Anchors us in the possibility of purpose in spite of the vast unknowing of our lives.

I am no musician. I have only words and a heart filled with child-wonder as I close my eyes and hear again this story of the beginning, of nothing to something, of chaos to order, of darkness and light, of stars in the night and sun for day bright. Waters above and waters below, the words of God drawing them apart, pulling the light from the dark. Blessing, always blessing. And God said it was, and it was. Good.

TRAVELING MERCY

Dear one,
The world wasn't,
Then it was.
You weren't,
But now you are.
And we are together
In time and space,
A continuum
Of relationship and glory
Forming,
Shaping,
Calling forth.
And I said.
And it is so.
Join me
In this act
Of creation.

NOTE TO SELF

Live life. Today.

DECEMBER 2

COMMUNICATION CAMPAIGN

In the beginning God (prepared, formed, fashioned, and)
created the heavens and the earth.

—GENESIS 1:1 AMP

In the beginning, God created. God cooked up the most massive communication campaign ever undertaken. God, out of endless and mind-blowing ideas of form and function, created.

Today, we recognize the miracle of the earth. Today, we know that the sun is a miracle, all twenty-seven million degrees Fahrenheit at its core, and that the moon hanging in the sky circles us while we circle the sun, helping to keep our world leaning, spinning, and orbiting perfectly for our ecosystems. We understand that no other planets in our solar system have the right conditions for our kind of life, because of extreme temperatures.

We know these awe-filled facts, after scientists studied and astronauts flew and satellites surveyed. Because people studied, experimented, gathered data, and interpreted that data, we know.

But we still can't replicate it.

In the beginning, God created the heavens and the earth. The rest of the chapter tells us *what* God created, but, with the exception of one or two details, not *how* God created it. And people get so hung up on *how* God created that they can't retrace their steps to the beginning, to the gargantuan miracle, and to the *why* behind the miracle.

Once the earth and the heavens were not. Now they are. It seems that here the creationists and the evolutionists agree, the camps of old earth/young earth, big bang or blow up or mind-boggling creativity. Once the earth was not. Now it is.

To focus the telescope a little tighter, earth was not and now is because God *created*. Most creativity, yours and mine, starts with something already in existence, and then remakes, reshapes, and re-forms that old something into a new something. Creativity is in some ways a recycling or reimagining of what currently exists. New forms for all those scraps, those leftovers. New uses.

As someone who has refashioned the same fabric for curtains in three or four homes, I appreciate the economy of reusing. But in the beginning, God created from nothing. God reused nothing. God started fresh. God created form from formlessness.

And while scientists, and you and I, cannot explain God—if we could, how would this Being be God?—there is a core longing for God, for someone or something outside of ourselves, so that we are not trapped in our own powerlessness. If we are all there is, then any purpose to our lives is elusive or temporal at best, a dead-end at worst. (Take that literally, if you like.)

So if this is all a communication campaign, what is the message? Earth, after all, was not the point of its creation.

We were. Planning to create us with such a longing, God started the whole ball rolling. Or spinning. Or orbiting. From formlessness, from void, from nothing God created. Not for an experiment in creativity. "Wow, let's see what happens if we do *this*."

The Creator designed for you and me. Without humanity, earth was an exercise in creativity or a giant science experiment. I look around at the blustering day, just another polar vortex day in the suburbs. I stand on a chair at the window to see as far as possible, through the swirling snow and the smoke puffing from chimneys and snaking horizontally in the blowing.

I wait for a minute with the thought: This was for me. For you. I cart out my list of fears, the unknowns and what-ifs. If God created the heavens and the earth for the purpose of placing us atop its glorious and variegated surface, why am I afraid?

We must talk ourselves off the ledge of fear. We are the works of God's hands, God's handiwork. Through the Artist, the art comes to life.

God purposed this earth with us in mind. From formlessness to no fear. From pain to purpose? No problem. That kind of creativity is a cinch to God.

TRAVELING MERCY

Dear one,
Come away from the edge of fear.
Stand on your chair
At the window on the world
And see.
I didn't go to all this trouble
Just for my creativity's sake.
Let me repurpose your pain,
Start a communication campaign,
Draw others back
From the ledge of fear
To the edge of their seats
With meaning.
So start communicating.

NOTE TO SELF

How can God repurpose my pain?

DECEMBER 3

A LONG COMFORT

In the beginning God . . .
—GENESIS 1:1

Finding our way is at first logistical. For many of us, just trying to make it through the day at hand. Or to shake free of yesterday. The first four words of the Bible comfort me deeply: "In the beginning God." Comforting, because long before we began, God. Because when there is none of me left, none of you left, to offer others, we can still move to this place: "In the beginning God." God in the beginning, God now, God forever.

If I return to the beginning of my day—or to the beginning of any other point in my life, like my career as a mother or my marriage—in the beginning, God. If I return to the beginning of my college years or high school days or the awkward, awful beginning of middle school: In the beginning, God.

Before I was, God.

In the beginning of our journey, however wayward or doglegged it seems, in the beginning, God. Whatever the path, God in the beginning.

And so it is for all of us. Before that crisis, that pain, that destruction or self-destruction—in the beginning, God.

Jews use the Hebrew name for God, *Hashem*, the Name, because *YHWH* (meaning "God was, God is, God always will be") is too holy to say. God is timeless, infinite. Since God was, is, and always will be, then the fact of God's presence changes everything.

Because in the beginning of each day or chapter or season or breath, we were not alone. We have been companioned by God, loved by God, cared for by God. Whether we felt alone or not—and it is important to identify those alone times, because they tell us about our abandonment fears and experiences, and are all very real—we were not alone. Others perhaps left us alone, the night thick about our souls, but that is not the whole truth. Because in the beginning, God.

So it follows that if "in the beginning God," and if every day and every moment and every breath represents a beginning, then, right now, this very moment, in our deepest distress or highest infatuation or soul-cleaving pain—God. In that beginning? God.

In the formlessness of our journey, in the dark creeping void of confusion or betrayal? In the beginning, right now and right then, God. In the simmering abyss of painful relationships, in the discouragement of toil and trouble, in the beginning, right now, God.

In the delight of a new love, in the beginning, God. In the wedding bells trilling from the spires, in the birth of a child, in the beginning, God.

In the troubling dissolution of hope, in the crumbling of vows, in others' breaking of faithfulness in our lives or us breaking it in theirs, even then: in the beginning, God.

Wherever we find ourselves, we return to this beginning point. Daily, weekly, however often we need to be reminded of the truth: in the beginning, God.

God in the beginning. God right now. God always.

And there, in that truth, we find a deep comfort. The facts of our lives—this happened, that happened, here we were hurt, there we lived great joy, here we were lost, there we were found—the facts of our lives speak only a shadow of the greater truth of our lives: In the beginning, God.

TRAVELING MERCY
Dear one,
In the beginning
I . . .
I was.
I am.
I always will be.
At work on your behalf,
Your good at the core of my intentions,
You at the heart of my actions
And my presence.
In the beginning, I, God,
And in the beginning I, God, with you.
So it is.
So it was.
So it will always be.
In the beginning.
In the now.
In the forever.
I, God.

NOTE TO SELF
Hope from the beginning and hope again.

CREATIVE INVITATION

In the beginning God created.

—GENESIS 1:1

Today I lay on my back on the wooden Murphy-style bed piano-hinged from the wall. Overhead, three hand-peeled pine tree trunks reach from one side to the other of the small one-room camp. My gaze travels: the windows that had been so carefully imagined, drawn on paper, redrawn, then imagined again—now perfectly placed to ensure light, ventilation, and a view of the woods and water and sky outside. The moon at night, the brilliant stars poking holes in the darkness, and the sun breaking over the horizon and shattering the darkness.

Every inch had been thought through: the insulation, thick on the inside of the walls, covered with plywood, waiting for paneling some day distant. The cabinets placed high above the twin bed frames that hide in the walls, but not too high for us to reach. Sturdy, welcoming, bright with natural light and a soft heater quiet in the background. The wide, open-armed porch surrounding the four walls with room enough for sixty kids to sleep in sleeping bags around the perimeter of the deep porch way.

My husband sleeps on the slim plank bed across from me, and I wait and watch for his eyes when he awakens. He does and finds me watching him, and I hope he sees my love there in that moment.

Later, we sit side-by-side in chairs, looking out the double-wide patio doors at the grounds, so recently cleared by the felling of bug-infested trees, the brush hauled tree by tree by my husband to a pile, and then chipped.

I look at him again, our hands clasped between us.

"How does it feel, to be here, in this place? This place that you dreamed of and then built?"

His dark eyes gleam and, if I'm not mistaken, take on a damp sheen. His smile broadens as wide as the porch. "It feels good." It is a full, replete statement in an overused word. But then, slowly, with space between each word, "It feels good to share it with someone." His hand tightens on mine. And then his smile takes over the room.

Yes. The ah-ha: creating and then inviting another into the fullness of that creation.

He never built this for himself. He could have tent-camped. But every minute of his labor, with every nail he purchased and pounded, with every beam he aligned, he thought not about his own enjoyment. He thought about the people who would share it with him.

He built it for *us*. To share. To laugh, love, create, rest, recover, recreate, refill.

Surely this is at the heart of the heavens and the earth, the "God created" of Genesis 1.

And why?

To share life with us. To invite us into life and joy and beauty and rest.

And at the heart of that?

Love. I see it in my husband's eyes, and I see it in my God's creation, wrapping around me like the arms of the porch outside.

TRAVELING MERCY

Dear one,
At the heart of creation,
One word:
Love.
And another word:
Sharing.
Love is made to share,
And this world
I created to share with you.
Creation without love
Isn't creation,
And love without creation
Isn't really love.
So take care what you create.
And I hope you catch
My heart.
Everything around you
Is because
I love you.
I hope you enjoy it with me
As much as I enjoy
You in this world.

NOTE TO SELF

Created with love, to love.

THE START OVER

In the beginning . . .

—Genesis 1:1

"In the beginning." Five syllables of hope. We all have beginnings. We all began somewhere. Whether we like our beginnings or not, whether we like our family who began us, we have beginnings.

Why is this hopeful? Why does this little phrase offer us hope?

A woman once told me, with haunted grief, that her date the night before had moved much faster than she wanted, than she expected. She felt ashamed and brokenhearted.

We were quiet together for a moment as those feelings seeped through her.

And then I said, "Today is a new day. A new beginning. You get to start over." Her sorrow and repentance over the sin was all God needed to see. Fully forgiven, she could figure out better boundaries for her relationships and learn to communicate them better to her date.

A new beginning. Every single day, a new start. Once brought to Christ, we can leave our guilt over our own sin in

God's hands, the one who "In the beginning" created. We don't need to mess with it for a minute longer than it takes to turn it over and seek forgiveness.

This triplet works no matter what we carry with us, no matter what we've stored in our backpacks. In my own satchel, I have found loss. I can grieve that, one more time, and then ask God to start me over. If the loss resurrects itself, we repeat the process. One day the "In the beginning" will be brand new. It will stick, for forever, over that one-time loss.

Maybe you find anger in your carry-on luggage. Well, dig out the root of that anger and then haul that dirt ball to God. Most anger entwines itself around our abandonment issues, our longings to be loved and cared for, protected. Feel it, really feel it, and then, "In the beginning." Maybe it's unforgiveness toward another. People's painful or mean or ugly behavior toward us is costly. What has it cost you? Our souls need to know that we notice and honor ourselves enough to consider that costliness. And then, "In the beginning."

Perhaps you have stashed disappointment. Feel it, enumerate those disappointments, and then, "In the beginning." Whatever and however you felt waking up, stay on the path of newness. And start your day with a fresh "In the beginning." Otherwise, our days are constantly dragged down by our stale luggage.

Sometimes, I don't want to start fresh. I want to carry around the hurt or anger or loneliness or disappointment like a medal of honor, so people notice and caretake. That's good to recognize in ourselves as well, but requires a little bit of tough love toward ourselves. C. S. Lewis said sometimes we need to tell our feelings where to get off. And then we review the truth, once more.

In the beginning. Today. A new start.

TRAVELING MERCY
Dear one,
In the beginning
I created,
And you can return to that beginning
Day after day.
Each day a new day.
Yesterday gone,
Today shiny new.
But only if you work the plan
And release yesterday
From your hands
And honor your feelings
Without being owned by them.
And then bring it all to me,
And we,
Together,
Begin again.
In the beginning.
Today.

NOTE TO SELF
Empty the backpack of yesterday. Start again today.

THE CREATIVE LIFE

In the beginning God created.

—GENESIS 1:1

God initiated creativity, back in the beginning of the beginning. This precedent makes me question creativity in our own lives. Immediately, perhaps, we protest, "Wait, no, no, no. I'm not creative. That's entirely not me." We throw our hands in the air and flail a bit, as though to ward off a disease or an eighth-grade art class assignment.

Maybe you don't love glue guns and Popsicle sticks. Do they even make pipe cleaners anymore? So quilting isn't your thing. (I always first spell that word with a G, so it reads, *guilting,* which autocorrect hates and which always garners me a bright squiggly red underline. But, guilting is about right, when it comes to crafts and me.) I'm not a gourmet cook, I don't paint, and repurposing now simply means composting. Which is perhaps a good place to put biodegradable failed craft projects. And I have never, not once ever in my entire online pseudo-social life, looked at Pinterest.

No more guilting allowed. Just because we don't major in fine arts and don't compose music, just because we aren't into home decorating and don't create awesome art out of driftwood doesn't mean we aren't creative or we can't live creatively.

Creativity doesn't imply brilliance, supreme gifting, or Pulitzer Prize genius. It just means to do something original. Something uniquely . . . well, uniquely you.

So who else could possibly do that? Absolutely no one. You are the only you, so anything you do is specific to you and therefore inherently creative.

Let's reconsider creativity as repurposing: finding new uses for stuff. Like my compost, a new use for organic matter, is repurposed in its new decomposing format to feed plants (and the occasional raccoon). What if we find a new use for something old in our personal lives, or a new response to an old stimulus? Then, each day isn't just maintaining, but a bringing forth of something new.

My friend Maggie, for instance, endured more psychological pain than should be permissible. An unstable home life led her to seek comfort wherever possible. Alcohol and drugs became her go-to sustaining tool, along with promiscuity. After several abortions, she learned she carried another baby and this time, decided to change her life. She got clean and sober, a miserable, painful, and ongoing journey. Raising the baby alone created incredible instability with her hand-to-mouth income. But she started listening to her gifts and began writing. She inched toward faith as a result of the Twelve Steps, and found Jesus.

Now a successful writer, she has a dynamic covert ministry to prisoners at some of the worst penitentiaries in America.

She teaches writing and English, and learns their stories. Most inmates are lifers, but her heart, with its own life sentence, draws her there to offer hope in the darkness.

She found her way because of God's hand in her life, powerful personal choices, and discipline. But she also found her way as she allowed God to reach past her fear and lead her into others' dark places. The light she shines reminds people they can find their way too. They may never be released from prison, but they can live free in their hearts. And help others en route.

Love as a creative response to pain.

It sure beats guilting. And glue guns.

TRAVELING MERCY
Dear one,
You don't have to create a whole world,
But when you love
You do create a world
Of acceptance and hope.
So glue-gun through your days,
With the binding texture
Of love and laughter,
Of hope and acceptance,
And see what creativity
Is set in motion
In this spinning world.
Maybe they're right after all:
Love makes the world go 'round.

NOTE TO SELF
Love as a creative response.

DECEMBER 7

NO APOLOGIES

First this: God created the Heavens and the Earth—
all you see, all you don't see.

—GENESIS 1:1 MSG

In the beginning, God created the heavens and the earth. The word used here for God, *Elohim*, means the one true God. Other religions try to convince us of the existence or validity of their gods by establishing where those gods started, how they got their beginning.

But not the Hebrew God. Not the Christian God. How did God get here? If we are really talking about the real God, then, how could we possibly know where God came from, how God came to be? To need to define that, as other religions do, seems to be a mark of defeat for the power of the god in question.

Our Bible is unapologetic about God's existence. God was, God is, and God always will be. These are entirely necessary qualities, defining and determining qualities, for God to be God. The little-G gods can't pull off that continuity.

"In the beginning God created the heavens and the earth" (Gen 1:1) offers certainty about our eternal God. God was, is, always will be. So we don't have to worry about being lost, because God is still God, because God always is. God never *wasn't*, however we feel emotionally, spiritually, or relationally.

This does wonders for abandonment issues, for the times when we feel ignored, forgotten, devalued, or slighted in some way. If God is and always was and always will be, then we're never alone, never forgotten. Further, our presence here on this earth determines without equivocation our value. God declares us worthwhile or humans would not exist.

In turn, that helps when we examine the news and flinch at the ever-present evil in the headlines: the act of creation declares the worth of that creation. In spite of heinous crimes, people themselves have value in God's sight. Their actions do not reflect their Creator; rather, their presence confirms the Creator and their own value.

Surely this softens our heart toward people accused or convicted of terrible things. Their actions in this world make another, far different but vital-to-understand statement: They are broken in significant ways, separated from the God who made them.

Everyone, on the front page and on the front line and in the front of our mind, reflects these truths. We are created by God. We are broken by life and act out our brokenness. We are separated from God. However, we are loved in spite of and in the midst of our brokenness. Aloneness is a lie. We are never alone.

We know this, because in the beginning, God created the heavens and the earth. In the beginning, God always was. And we have been in God's heart from the beginning, the God who said, "Before I formed you in the womb I knew you, before you were born I set you apart" (Jer. 1:5).

We can move ahead then, on a path we do not see, knowing that the God who formed the world formed us and has set us apart. We can move away from the pain of disappointment in others and ourselves, away from our abandonment disposition and abandoning behaviors, and toward God. Embraced by God, companioned by God, we help others find their way out of loneliness into relationship. One more great conversion—pain to purpose.

TRAVELING MERCY

Dear one,
Because I am,
I was,
I have always been
And always will be,
Your worth is secured.
Before you were born,
Before you were formed,
I knew you;
I declared your value.
Your brokenness,
Others' brokenness,
Is not the final word.
I am the Word,
and I declare
That you are loved.
Because you are.
You wouldn't exist
Unless I thought you mattered.
I was, I am, I always will be.
And so is my care for you.

NOTE TO SELF

Move from loss toward God and toward others.

DECEMBER 8

HOPE IN THE DARK

Now the earth was formless and empty, darkness was over the
surface of the deep, and the Spirit of God was hovering over the waters.

—GENESIS 1:2

Formless. Empty. Darkness. These words bring a brooding
fearfulness to this verse. They strike far too close to home.
So many lives feel as formless as a windsock in a vacuum,
deflated and useless. Or used up. Emptiness is a terrible sense,
with our lacks creeping around in the basement of our soul: lack
of value, identity, purpose, hope. Insignificance is corrosive, and
so much of our society's ills can be traced to these three words.

And that word, *deep*. It's a terrifying word in and of itself,
even without the others in its wake. The watery deep envelopes
all that is, a primeval substance, pre-creation. This is the word
in Genesis 7:11 at the flood, when "all the springs of the great
deep burst forth." There is an out-of-control, terrifying, powerful
essence to this deep. It is the unknown in all our lives, this watery
deep, with frightening, lurking danger beneath the surface.

From orphanage to classroom, from childcare to college, from
cradle to cap and gown until the coffin, much of our drivenness
and our deflation are due to the formless, empty, dark deep that
we either battle or succumb to throughout our lives.

But any snapshot reveals only partial truth. A picture of you or me on one day, dressed up for a special occasion, a glowing image of health and happiness, does not reveal that we awoke with half a heart, the other half left with a child in another state, a loved one on a ventilator, an empty wedding ring finger, a womb empty yet again. We musn't stop at half a verse, half a day, half a heart, or half a life. That's not the whole story.

Thankfully, God did not leave us in this formless void, this terrifying, inexpressible meaninglessness. "The Spirit of God was hovering over the waters." I feel almost breathless to read this, and to rest there, bobbing on my watery deep, panting and grateful, these words a raft.

In fact, Genesis 1:2 is most hopeful, because God saw the nothingness, the emptiness, the lack of form, and still divined purpose in it all. More than that, God crafted, from this chaotic and unmade state of nothing, the world. Our world. The world where we would be shaped from dirt, then bone. The world where we would come to be.

Do you see, there, the centripetal pull? God hovered over the entire process, always at work, always transforming behind the scenes, pulling all to the center. Before there *were* any scenes, God was there. The nothingness is nothing to God.

So the feeling of being formless and void, of having a life without meaning or purpose? The questions of how life is valuable in the midst of pain, of isolation? The sometimes suffocating sense of loss or loneliness?

Read it again. From that dark formlessness, God created. Then, the Spirit hovered over the entire mass. And today, the Holy Spirit still hovers and beckons into life.

The formlessness, the void, the seeming lack of purpose, is really all part of God's creative process. God is constantly doing a new thing. In fact, take a peek at the next verse: "God said, 'Let there be light'" and the lights went up in the stadium of the universe. I can't wait to see what happens next. Meanwhile, our formless, deep, dark void is not the final state. Just wait. Creativity is on the way.

TRAVELING MERCY

Dear one,
In the beginning
I was.
In spite of the dark, the deep,
The formlessness
That feels like your life.
I am,
And I am throwing on the lights
And plying my creativity
To make a way for you.
You are significant
Or I would not have created
The world.
The nothingness
Is not the truth,
Because I am the God
Who transforms,
Shapes,
Creates.

NOTE TO SELF

Ask God to shape me.

NIGHT VISION

God saw that the light was good, and [God]
separated the light from the darkness.

—GENESIS 1:4

My soul hushes at the order of God's creative acts. God created light with the words, "Let there be." God liked it and declared it good. And then God separated the light from the darkness.

Wait. What? So before God separated the light from the darkness, the light was *part* of the darkness? Then, inherent in darkness is the fact of light. However dark life may seem, light is also present, part of the darkness.

And so the darkness is not in itself malevolent. It is not an abyss, an absence of hope.

My art teacher from junior high told us that black is the presence of all color. If you want black and don't have a little black rectangular patch in your watercolor kit, then just drag your wet brush through all the other colors (including white) and *voila!* Black.

So, all color is present in black—including white. Light is present, according to Genesis 1:3, in darkness. Light in darkness. White in black.

This is not a review of the principles of color. It is a review for life. The darkness can be excruciating—not only formless and void, but also seemingly endless and with no exit tunnel. The front page of the paper, the evening news, the round-the-clock reporting of darkness in this world: no end of darkness. No end.

And yet, if light is present in darkness, then we, with God's help, can extricate the light from the dark. We can find the light.

What can the darkness do? Plants tell you (if they can speak, and they can, because growth or its opposite is their way of speaking) that in the darkness they will strive for growth, seeking the light desperately. So the darkness can offer growth if we look.

What do we learn here in the dark? What do we learn about ourselves, our fears, our pain? What do we learn about others? About God?

Do we simply bide our time, waiting for the darkness to end? Or is it possible to live in the dark for a season, to name the darkness and then work daily and even minute by minute to find the light in that dark? We don't have to figure and finagle our way out of the darkness on our own. Nor do we try to eradicate the darkness for all time—as though that were even an option, short of heaven.

Rather, we seek the light in the midst of the right now of darkness, in our current darkness.

And if we need night vision, well, good news. The Scriptures tell us in 1 John 1:5 that "God is light; in him there is no darkness at all."

TRAVELING MERCY

Dear one,
There is darkness
And there is light,
And I am in the midst of both,
Right in the middle of your darkness.
Name the darkness,
But do not give the darkness power
To overwhelm you.
Rather, name that darkness
And invite me
To reveal the light
Hidden in the dark recesses
Of life in a hurting world.
Your world.
Others' world.
I've done it from the beginning,
Separating dark from light.
And your life
Will prove the rule,
Not be the exception.

NOTE TO SELF

Search the darkness for light. Grow in that direction.

WORD POWER

God said, "Let there be . . ."
—GENESIS 1:3

Ten times in Genesis 1, we read, "God said." Each of those instances is a declaration, a decree. When God speaks, action results: The winds obey, the waters gather themselves, and the darkness separates from light. God speaks, and the world forms, and re-forms. God says, and the elements snap to attention and assume their orders.

Words, God's words, equal power. The creative essence of God's authority brings into being that which was not. When God speaks, God creates.

Is it possible that we bring such power to our words as well? When we speak, we create: We create an environment, an atmosphere, whether of love and acceptance or of judgment, whether of passivity or of responsibility. Our words bring power: power to heal and power to tear down, power to give life and power to give death, power to form and power to transform.

Writers know that there are good words and there are great words, specific words that say exactly what needs to be said, with an economy of space. A "red, boiled-wool coat" is always better than a "coat." Words offer a visual to the invisible. They create an entire world for people to inhabit—read a novel or watch a good movie and see if those words didn't whisk you away to a new space, a different world. I've known travel writers who've never traveled to the places they feature in articles, but they write with such beauty that they recreate those places with savory images, with all the senses awakened. They've created a world with their words.

When God speaks, God creates. But is it also true that when God creates, God speaks? I look at the stars, piercing the sky's dark blanket with minute holes of light. I gaze at the crisp frost that outlines the thin fingers of the dark and naked trees, those dainty flakes of freeze clothing them in ethereal beauty. I marvel at the painted horizon in the morning and in the evening. And if God speaks in the act of creation, what does he say?

God creates and says, "I love you. You matter. You are the reason I gave form to this world, and you are the reason I flung the stars into space and tethered them by the force it would take eons for you to discover. You are the reason the grass grows green, and you are the reason the flowers bloom. You are the reason I create."

Because God loves us.

There is no other explanation for creation. Because God could live in the midst of the invisible for forever, eternity future, just as in eternity past. But God chose to create with words of authority and chose to speak our world into existence. God gave it form and function and placed us within it, in order to tell us just one thing. Just one, critical message, essential to life, as essential to life as the sun: "I love you."

So today, I practice creating a world with my own words and inviting others into that God-blooming sphere. Like, "Thank you." And how about, "I love you, too"? Season with a smile and the sky's the limit. Heaven too.

TRAVELING MERCY
Dear one,
I said, "Let there be . . ."
And there was.
There is.
Look around.
Look up.
Let all the created order
Lead you to me,
To my love,
My heart for you,
My hopes for you.
I love you,
I shaped you,
I spoke you into being.
Now use your words
To speak new worlds,
New love,
New hope
Into life.

NOTE TO SELF
Choose life-giving words today.

THE SKY IS CALLING

God spoke: "Sky! In the middle of the waters; separate water from water!" God made sky. He separated the water under sky from the water above sky. And there it was: he named sky the Heavens.

—GENESIS 1:6–8 MSG

Today, the sky alternates between the color of old weathered wood and flashes the shade of a bright bluebird wing. How I take for granted the sky, the huge unsupported cathedral of the heavens above. I don't quake in fear that the sky is falling. Neither do I always see the sky as an icon that leads me toward God, that speaks to me of God's presence in our lives.

God set this marker in the sky, spoke it into existence, and vaulted over us this dome. And forevermore the sky reminds us of God. Think of it: We look at the sky daily, unless we live in a cave or a basement or under water, and every single glance upward is an opportunity to jog our memory about God.

The sky reminds us not just of God's creative power, of the brilliant plan of intervention between the waters above and the waters below. It jogs our memory of God's presence with us and high intentions for us. "For as high as the heavens are above the earth, so great is his love for those who fear him" (Ps. 103:11). So great, so vast, so high, so unending as the sky— God's love for us is that kind of huge.

And the firmament also inspires such confidence. When the waves that crash on life's shore wash up over our hopes and dreams, obliterating our fragile pathways, we stand on solid ground. God knows the end from the beginning, and we see it in the skies. Vaulted thoughts, God has of us. "As the heavens are higher than the earth, so are my ways higher than your ways and my thoughts than your thoughts" (Isa. 55:9).

This floods me with relief. We are not on our own, after all. We are not washed away on the tides of trauma. No. Because God's love is higher than the heavens above us and wider than the vast expanse that arches over our heads. God's purposes for us are far loftier than we could imagine or dream. And they are larger and higher and kinder than any broken interpretation we experience here below.

Because not everyone lives with freedom from fear, with peace when glancing at the sky overhead. In far too many parts of the world, the sky *is* falling. Bombs dropping from the air. Guided missiles exploding in streets and buildings. People's lives and hopes blasted apart in an instant as the skies rain death.

As we watch the firmament and cast our gaze toward the heavens, may the vault overhead secure our hearts to God and to prayer for those in this world who live in fear of the falling sky. The sky is calling. May God use us to bring peace on earth. To pause, to pray, to offer practical assistance. And to wage peace against war.

TRAVELING MERCY
Dear one,
Look above
And look toward me.
Then look around you
At all those who fear.
The sky is calling.
My love is greater than the sky,
Greater than their fear.
Today.

NOTE TO SELF
Called to prayer and to peace.

DECEMBER 12

UNFINISHED

God made the vault and separated the water under the vault from
the water above it. And it was so. God called the vault "sky."

—Genesis 1:7–8

The second day is the only day of creation where God didn't
pronounce the day's work good. There was evening and there
was morning the second day, but nowhere does God say, "Yes,
good, well done. I like this a lot." Why might that be? Some
rabbis refuse to comment on this missing declaration because
God said nothing to clue them in. Others boldly suggest that
since division and strife destroy relationships, the division of
the waters, the schism, was not good, not yet, and God couldn't
say it was good.

What we know for sure is that God wasn't finished, and
God is a finisher. On day four the sun went into the sky, and it
was just right. The moon, too. When the waters were contained
and the land appeared on day three, God nodded and said,
"Yes, good." All the other "goods" were ready to rock and
roll. They denoted, as Rabbi Rashi says, a finished creation.[1]
But that schism between earth and heaven? Silence.

God isn't just a yes God. "It's all good," people shrug and
say in the midst of disappointment or outright tragedy. That's

a total lie. It isn't all good. God never said it was all good. God withheld that word on day two's unfinished work.

In reality, our lives contain many "not goods." There is no shame in saying, "Not good." In declaring that the brokenness isn't good, the pain isn't good. The schism isn't good.

Carry that reality further, however. It isn't good today. But the work of creation—God creating in us a new heart, God mending our broken hearts, God healing cracks in our soul and in our relationships—is ongoing. God didn't quit on day two, walking out on the job of the whole business of creation. No, God wasn't finished with the work of the waters and the sky on day two. But God could still call out the end of day two, "Evening and morning," something we have a hard time doing, even when we can declare it good. But if it's not good, all the harder not to just fix it no matter how long it takes right now.

So it is with us. We can be honest when someone says, "How are you?" The expected answer is, "Good." Or, grammatically correct, "Well. I am well, thank you." But this isn't honest, not always.

But it will be one day. And that is where we hang our hat of hope. Day two wasn't finished, but by day three, well, it was good.

Hold on for day three, friend. Don't be afraid of the not-goods. And don't give up. Day three is coming. And four, five, six, and, ah, blessed relief, day seven.

Then, we can say by faith, "It's not all good. Not yet. But it will be. Soon."

Good.

TRAVELING MERCY
Dear one,
It is not good.
Not everything is good.
So mind your words.
It will help you to mind your heart,
To pay attention
To the unfinished work within you.
Watch for the day two schisms and divisions
And trust me
To help establish unity.
In you.
Through you.
In this world.

NOTE TO SELF
Breech the schisms.

NOTE
1. Rabbi Nosson Scherman, *The Chumash: The Stone Edition with Complete Sabbath Prayers* (Brooklyn, NY: Mesorah Publications, 2000), 5.

DECEMBER 13

A HIGHER PURPOSE

Then God said, "Let the land produce vegetation:
seed-bearing plants and trees on the land."

—GENESIS 1:11

On a walk in the woods, my husband and I paused at the base of a ridge and stared up at a gigantic white pine, its long needles bunching together in clusters. The overall effect is soft and full, generous shade extending from sturdy, well-spaced branches. A good climbing tree, our kids would deem it. Tall enough for the eagles to hover over it, a possible nesting spot there in the distance.

The white pines in this forest outlasted the bug plague that devoured the spruce. Now, without the spruce, those majestic pines rise like statues with the space cleared of the weedy poplar trees as part of the forestry initiative. These mock birch trees will return in a few minutes, their hasty runner roots shooting just below the surface in all directions ensuring recurrence and fast, spindly growth. But they're no competition for the grandest trees in the forest.

This straight-backed pine on the crest has the advantage of placement, a high spot, easier access to the light. It towers from that place. But with height comes the companion, risk—

lightning, storms, and wind's bluster all threaten the tall tree's survival and growth. The soft green needles wave a victory flag. The elements have not overcome the tree.

Further on, another pine, also gigantic, looks like it has scoliosis with its twists and turns. We study this tree, its footing closer to sea level. The tree's determination to move ahead with life strikes us both.

We process this. Are the obstacles the point of the journey? As writers and storytellers and musicians, we find this appealing, a chord of creative fodder for the artistic mill.

But this idea is short-lived or at least shortsighted. Partly because it's dreadful to imagine that the obstacles are the whole point. Why go forward then? Why seek a work-around, like the tree with scoliosis? The obstacles cannot be the point and purpose of the journey. Obstacles by their very nature throw roadblocks into the path of a higher purpose.

The purpose of life is not the pain. The purpose is finding a way through the pain into the promise of becoming. Becoming what though? The biggest, stateliest tree in the forest?

No. The best you, the best me possible. The tree trunks tell a story, a life story, a long, many-chaptered saga. A story of obstacle and determination. A story of overcoming.

And so do our lives tell a story, the same story as that of the trees: obstacle, determination, overcoming. Becoming "mature, attaining to the whole measure of the fullness of Christ" (Eph. 4:13). If we keep focused on the purpose of our journey. Not a birch tree wannabe.

Overcoming leads to becoming.

TRAVELING MERCY

Dear one,
Your journey is yours alone,
But your purpose is the same
As those around you:
Become yourself,
Your best self possible
In spite of,
And in light of,
And maybe because of,
The obstacles in the way.
Do not lose your focus.
Do not despair.
Overcoming leads
To becoming.
So hold on;
I will help you climb.

NOTE TO SELF

Check focus: on the obstacle or on overcoming?

DECEMBER 14

LIGHT UP

"Let there be lights in the vault of the sky to
separate the day from the night."

—GENESIS 1:14

God, who is light, who dwells in inapproachable light, in whom is no darkness, and to whom the darkness is as light—this God, our God, the one true God, is not threatened by other lights.

We, of course—as we try to find our way, as we circle our gifts and talents and try to decide, with fear and trembling, how to develop them, how to grow into who we are created to be—find others' lights threatening. Overwhelming. Blinding, even. We wish, sometimes, they would dim their lights at appropriate times (as in, when we are present).

Most artists know there are others artisans far more accomplished, more celebrated, more rewarded than they themselves. Writers, too, realize there are plenty of books and articles filled with well-constructed sentences and paragraphs and thoughts, and that many or most of those are far better than they could ever write. Sculptors and architects study the greats before them, examine the Sistine Chapel's vast painted dome, and inspect the marble that held Michelangelo's

David. And these sculptors and architects know they cannot possibly compete with such masterpieces.

Regardless of our job descriptions, there are always lights far greater, far brighter than our own.

Then should our response be that we just don't light up at all? What if the lightning bug caught sight of the moon and said, "I absolutely cannot compete with that light"?

God, who lives in light, knew that life needs light. So God hung the sun in place, the moon, the thousands of stars that give light to the darkness. God wasn't threatened by light, but rather, shared that light. And then those lights functioned as only those lights are able to function. The moon doesn't try to be the sun or the stars. The stars don't attempt to compete with the sun—they have a different function than the sun.

Lights do what lights do: they shine; they illuminate; they bring life.

Part of finding our way, of moving from pain to purpose, is recognizing our own luminosity. We all have the ability to shine, as we are filled with the Light of the World. Didn't Jesus say, "I am the light of the world" (John 8:12)? And then—this threw the Jewish politicos back on their heels—that "you are the light of the world" (Matt. 5:14)? We share the light we're given by using the gifts we're given, however small those seem in comparison to the others shining in the celestial landscape about us. We are the light of the world as we fill ourselves with Christ's light, and offer that light to others as well.

Maybe it looks like lovingkindness. Or the gift of mercy. Or encouragement. Whatever the gifts God gives us, whatever light we have, that light we so shine. This little light?

Yes. That little light. My little light, and yours, too. Others may have spotlights, and mine may look like a birthday candle. Your light is perhaps an exploding, showering fireworks display.

Our task is not to compare ourselves to the stars and the sun and the moon around and over us. But to just shine.

Jesus said you're the light of the world. And no light, no life.

TRAVELING MERCY
Dear one,
Just shine;
That's all.
Don't compare,
Don't overcompensate,
Don't burn out,
Don't be afraid
To let your little light,
Or your big light,
Out into this world.
No matter what,
You reflect me.
So shine on.
Shine clear.
Shine as only you can.

NOTE TO SELF
Shine. Use all my lumens.

DESIGNER WEAR

"Let birds fly above the earth across the vault of the sky."

—GENESIS 1:20

The blue jay lands on the ground outside my window. Sharp bills grip a tiny purple berry. The bird throws back its head with its black mask and its slick-backed headpiece, and the dark ball dislodges and slides down the bird's handsome throat. The bird turns its attention to the base of the lilac bush, rummaging around the rusty remnants of autumn and uncovering a bright green leaf. Salad, anyone? Or a new winter lining for the nest, Mama?

A fierce parent, the blue jay dive-bombs anyone who happens close to its nest where young birds wait for wing strength. During flying lessons, the papa bird plays vigilant guard, taking potshots at too-close passersby. We have ducked and run for cover many times over the years when we wandered into flight school.

The brilliance of this one bird, just one bird of the ten thousand-some species identified—makes me stop for a minute, overwhelmed with the detail of the creation of this world. One bird, so ornate, with such striking and deliberate markings, survival skills, and protective instincts. Just one bird.

God's attention to detail inspires me. As I read Genesis 1–2, while considering all the details of my own life that overwhelm me, I feel the stays on my straitjacket begin to loosen. The anxiety that I carry with me like it's a second layer of skin—it begins to molt away.

A blue jay with its bandit face and vigilance over its young—how much more vigilant is God, over your life and over your heart? And over my own life and the state of my soul?

God is more vigilant than the highest heavens, vaulting over our insufficiencies and covering all our inadequacies and fears.

Not only that, but God made every winged bird according to its kind. Meaning, it is specifically designed for its particular style and gifts. The eagle's wings are perfect for an eagle's lifestyle. Just so, the sparrow's and chicken's wings. The albatross and the osprey, the brilliant parrot, and the miniature hummingbird: all just right for the jobs and lives they live.

If this is true for the ten thousand bird species, isn't it so for us as well? God formed our arms just the right length, our bodies the right height, and our gifts just perfect for the lives God invites us to live.

We can't waste time wishing for another's wingspan or feather color. There's no room for jealousy among the eagles and the blue jays—nor between you and me. Each of us, designed just right for our individual lives.

It's enough to make your heart—well, fly. Maybe that's part of soaring "on wings like eagles" (Isa. 40:31).

TRAVELING MERCY

Dear one,
Designed just so—
You and your neighbor
And the bird outside your window.
Designed specifically for your life
And your calling
And your needs
And your purpose.
Don't let worry
Clip your wings,
But rather
Launch off,
Secure in my calling,
My design.
It should be enough
To make your heart
Fly.

NOTE TO SELF

How do I live like a designer original?

THE RISK ANALYSIS

"Let us make mankind in our image."
—GENESIS 1:26

Consider that God out of sheer love chose to create a world from what wasn't. And to cover that world with water and land, mountains and grasses, ravines and plains. To plant trees of all varieties, fruit bearing and seed bearing. To add into the mix animals, the most wildly and widely varied selection of creatures imaginable. Then put some feathers on some thin little bones, invent wings, and *voila!* Send these bodies flying and flitting over the earth, delighting in the berries and the seeds. Then, here's a thought, how about something with scales and fins and a tail, something that will breathe water instead of air. And, oh, let's make these live in the water and give them all sorts of shapes and purposes, some with teeth and some without.

Such joy, this creation. Such color, variety, and glory, all representing facets of the creator God's infinite creativity.

It seems like a really good time in heaven, all things considered.

But something was missing. A decided dimension to the exploding creativity. Something with soul, something that

could be given a will and could choose to respond to the surrounding world, to all the color and glory. Something that could
decide about loving in return.

So in a supreme act of generosity and love, God scooped up
some dirt and shaped it into the form of a man. Two arms, two
legs, opposable thumbs, a heart, and a soul. The ability to choose:
to love, to leave, to obey, to disobey, to follow the Creator's way,
to follow his own way. And then, a woman, from the rib of the
man of dirt, a helper, because it wasn't and never would be
good to be entirely alone. Two human beings, made in God's
likeness, to complete and companion one another.

A supreme act of generosity? Yes. Because God knew the
risk involved in a creature who could choose love or hate, obedience or disobedience. God knew that real love could never be
forced, that coercion would always mean obligation rather than
freedom. That reciprocity had to be entirely voluntary.

Loving is *always* a risk. It was a risk during the early days
of the earth and of the first human beings. It is a risk now. To
love is to risk rejection, mockery, abandonment.

But not to love is a far greater risk. In not loving, we lose
the multi-dimensions of relationships: the joy, the delight, the
wonder. In not loving, we may stay safe, yes, but we also
remain unchanged by the dynamics of love, the give and take
required of relationship that leads us into growth. Wholeness
is so rarely accomplished in isolation.

Without relationship we are partial, rather than whole. Not
that others complete us, in the sense of our dependency on
them, but rather that relationships offer us the opportunity to
become better at loving, to grow in generosity. Better at

focusing not only on ourselves and our own needs and issues, but at opening up to others' needs.

By God's supreme act of generosity, we, too, can take the risk of loving. And generosity, rather than becoming a risk for us, actually becomes a means of growth and of moving toward wholeness. All part of finding our way.

It is better than we could ever have imagined.

But not to God. God knew, all along, what we have yet to fully embrace: The generosity of love can propel the world, change the world, heal the world, heal us.

TRAVELING MERCY

Dear one,
The joy of creation
Unparalleled but insufficient
Until I added you
To the mix
And threw in
The challenge of loving,
The bonus and benefit of loving.
We all win
When we choose love
In spite of the risks.
So today
I will love you,
And you in turn
Love others.
And no matter what,
We all win.

NOTE TO SELF

Love in spite of the risks.

TOO OLD FOR THAT

God blessed them and said to them, "Be fruitful."

—Genesis 1:28

This week, I passed an interstate billboard that shouted, "You're too old!" I'm sure a lot of people driving past either nodded their heads in agreement or shook them with vehemence. In a society that idolizes youthfulness, with a bazillion-dollar cosmetics industry, premature retirement options, and plastic surgeries rising, "You're too old," resonates.

But the subtext of that billboard got to me: "For a job you hate." The technical college in Indiana couldn't be more correct. To hate our jobs will decrease our life's joy, and it might make us too old too soon.

Leaving a job we loathe to do something we might love could be completely unsustainable. It could seem like a luxury we can't afford. People who wake up and leap out of bed with joy to go to work may be few. I thank God for the opportunity to work at something I enjoy, and I don't take it lightly. Sadly, I would guess that I am in the minority.

But maybe there is a workaround for all the work we don't like to do (and I won't lie to you, a lot of work involved in writing and speaking I am not fond of, like administrative tasks). If you wake up daily to a life you don't like, to work you can't stand, reconsider Genesis 1:28.

When God created people, the instructions were, "Be fruitful and increase in number; fill the earth and subdue it." The Hebrew defines the word *fruitful* as "bearing fruit" but also "to flourish." Jewish rabbis don't limit *flourishing* to only mean, "having children." This is good news for the 11 percent of women ages 15–44 in the United States who are unable to conceive or carry a baby to term, and for the 7 percent of men who have seen a fertility doctor in their lifetime.[1] But it is also wonderful to reconsider fruitfulness in light of our society, our economy, and relationship dynamics.

To be fruitful—to flourish—is expanded upon by rabbis to mean, "using one's gifts," whether intellectual, technical, artistic, or physical. Develop and use those gifts; flourish in the use of them. Write, paint, sculpt, draw, design, sew, think, invent, develop, and use your smarts for the good of the world and the glory of God.

What gifts or interests would you like to develop? Fruitfulness might just look like a night class in welding—a friend surprised everyone when she enrolled. Another learned to make jewelry in her off hours, since her job was just about to kill her but she couldn't afford to leave. Another started watercolor painting and has since won awards in shows for her work.

One man started a bike repair business, then a biking club. A man joined who had lost his leg after combat. The business owner invented a modification that allowed the veteran to ride. And ride he did—all the way to the Paralympics, where he won a bronze medal.

There is no limit to the many displays of fruitfulness. This becomes especially clear as we consider what would ultimately become God's mandate many years later to Abraham: God would bless Abraham and make him a blessing (see Gen. 12:1–4). Fruitfulness that grows our soul, and our relationship with God, can in turn multiply in this world by gracing others.

The billboard is right. You're too old . . . to hate what you do. So do what you love, or learn to love something you do. And everyone wins.

TRAVELING MERCY
Dear one,
Be fruitful.
Multiply.
It all adds up
To faithfulness
And to my glory
As people see you
Developing your gifts
And expanding your reach
With my arms
Through you
Into the world.
So be fruitful.
Flourish.
Leave the higher math
To me.

NOTE TO SELF
Conversion effect: languishing into flourishing?

NOTE
1."Infertility FAQs," Center for Disease Control and Prevention, accessed April 21, 2015, http://www.cdc.gov/reproductivehealth/ Infertility/index.htm.

SPEAKING INTO BEING

And it was so.

—GENESIS 1:7, 9, 11, 15, 24, 30

Genesis 1 tells us a great deal about God, about creation, about the power of words. God said, "Let there be," and there was. Light, darkness—separated; sky, earth, waters—separated. Plants, seeds, water-life, air-life, earth-life. But this chapter also tells us about hope, about speaking into being that which is not—at least, that which is not *yet*.

God said, "Let there be," and there was. Seven times Genesis 1 says, "And it was so." If God's words have such power, then what words might God be speaking into your life right now? "Let there be _____." Fill in the blank, and then say that sentence aloud, pray it, as often as you need to. Draw more blanks and fill them all in throughout your day, and in your long nights of darkness.

Maybe you need peace, to hear and receive it, to have it spoken into your life right now. If the God who created the possibility for the universe and called forth peace between the elements of the cosmos, if that same God has invited us to be people of peace—what does Psalm 147:14 say? God "grants peace to your borders and satisfies you with the finest of wheat"—well, then, we can say, "Let there be peace, Lord." Peace is part of God's plan for us. "If it is possible, as far as it depends on you, live at peace with everyone" (Rom. 12:18). Second Thessalonians 3:16 says, "Now may the Lord of peace himself give you peace at all times and in every way." Then we can rightly ask, "Let there be peace, God. Fill me with peace. Speak your peace into me as you spoke it into creation."

Maybe you are in dire need of some joy. "Restore to me the joy of your salvation and grant me a willing spirit, to sustain me" (Ps. 51:12). How about saying this, then? "God, let there be joy in me this day. Please, speak joy into my soul." Two hundred forty-two verses declare joy into us and God brings joy as a gift for us. Pray them, and invite God to speak them into your soul and voice and the works of your hands.

Or perhaps right now fear tunnels holes like a hornet's nest. The opposite of fear is trust, and the psalmist said, "Trust in the LORD with all your heart, and do not rely on your own understanding" (Prov. 3:5 NET). When I'm afraid, I'm trusting *my* understanding of the situation, rather than God's. My own understanding is always going to be unenlightened and shortsighted, but not God's.

Let there be light, let there be life, let there be the water of tears and kindness in our lives. Let there be vision, let there be passion, let there be relationship in our lives. Let there be beauty, let there be fruit, let there be faithfulness. Let there be hope. "May the God of hope fill you with all joy and peace as you trust in him, so that you may overflow with hope by the power of the Holy Spirit" (Rom. 15:13).

Let there be, God, let there be. Please speak it into our lives as you spoke it into this very world around us.

TRAVELING MERCY

Dear one,
I spoke
And it was so.
Let me speak now
Into your life,
And it will be so as well.
Let there be light,
Let there be fruitfulness,
Let there be creativity and joy
And peace and wellness.
My words are filled
With all I want to give you.
So I say,
Let there be.
Will you join me?
Together we will see
My words
Come to fulfillment
For you.
In you.
Through you.
Into this world.

NOTE TO SELF

Take inventory: Let there be . . . what?

THE DECLARATION

Day after day [the heavens] pour forth speech;
night after night they reveal knowledge.

—Psalm 19:2

"Use your words," parents sometimes tell their children. Their cranky or fighting children, their whining children, their plaintive, sobbing children who refuse bedtime but are too tired to sit up. "Use your words." *Please* use your words. Some parents teach their infants sign language so that the babies learn to show what they need rather than cry helplessly, which leads to helpless feelings in the parents and sometimes frustration and even anger. Words help. So parents teach signs for words like hungry, more, please, thank you, all done.

The Scriptures tell us that God used words to create the world: "God said." They also tell us that Jesus, the Word, sustains all things by the power of his word (see Heb. 1:3), and that the world around us clues us into something about its Creator: "The heavens declare."

Declare what? The glory of God. The earth, the sky, the waters above and below, the separation of dark from light— these all speak, tell, shout of the glory of God. The sun rising in the morning and setting in the evening: It's a live stream of God's glory. The moon at night, "the lesser light," speaking with its reflection; God is glorious. God, the God of glory. Glorious God.

The heavens and the earth and the flowering plants and the fruit-bearing trees and the brilliant under-the-sea life, seen only by God until fairly recent history. Glory, glory, glory. *Glory* seems to be a word we should reserve for God, only for God. Any other use pales. Like the halogen light over my head, powered by an outside generator in this camp building: that light is helpful, it is brilliant, it would blind me if I looked straight into it. But it is not the sun, doesn't remotely compare with the sun except that this light is bright, and it breaks up the darkness.

But the sun? All one million degrees of it, perfectly placed in the only spot that would sustain life? One degree closer and earth is torched. One degree farther away and this world as we know it becomes a ball of ice.

So the light? Nice, helpful. The sun? Brilliant, perfect.

Glory? Only God. Only for God. All else is reflected glory or perhaps like a piece of a stained glass window, nice, bright, colorful, but not the whole.

The earth uses its words to speak, and it speaks the language of beauty. But that word, *beauty*, feels weak. The earth speaks in the language of . . . glory. God's glory, reflected here, pointing us toward heaven, toward God the creator, who created this place to share with us.

The heavens declare. And we declare. We use our words, but we also use our lives to declare. We live in such a way that our lives, words, and actions make God look good.

God's glory.

TRAVELING MERCY
Dear one,
A million degrees
Is not too much
To express to you
The message from the very beginning:
In the beginning
I created
Because I love,
And now all that I create declares
My glory.
Is that what your life
Speaks to the world?
My glory.

NOTE TO SELF
Use my words and life to speak God's glory.

ALL IN A DAY'S WORK

> By the seventh day God had finished all the work he had
> been doing; so on the seventh day he rested from all his work.
>
> —GENESIS 2:2

The roofer climbs down from his high perch and puts away his tools. "Let's call it a day." And he packs up his toolbox and heads home.

Call it a day.

As we read in the creation account, God called forth each day, and then called the work complete for that day. There was evening and there was morning—the first day, the second day, the third, clear to day six. Each day, God called it a day, deciding that was enough work for that particular day.

But we, in this day and age, find it hard to call it a day. Maybe your days and nights are all the same, and you work nonstop around hearth and home, neighborhood and church. Maybe you punch out of your day job, calling it a day there, but then there's the second shift, the work at home, the kids, the volunteering, and the house and yard. Call it a day? How about a day and most of a night, and then we can "call it a day"?

No way can we ever call it a day and just relax in the thought, "Well, we've done enough this day. Sufficient to the day is the work thereof," or something like that. It's never sufficient. There is always, always, always more work than there is day, so we steal from the night, and then before we lose ourselves in REM sleep, it's day all over again.

Surely God knew this, back in the beginning. That we would struggle to complete our day, day would then compete with night, and we would end up a people with either sleep deprivation or insomnia. Or both, which is a little bit of a catch-22.

The Scriptures tell us, "By the seventh day God had finished all the work he had been doing; so on the seventh day he rested from all his work" (Gen. 2:2). We sure aren't God, so does that let us off the hook? Since only God could possibly finish all the work necessary in the allotted timeframe of day, we're free to work and worry day and night? So we can never really "call it a day" in the true sense? We turn on all our inventions of light that compete with the rhythm of day and night, and keep plugging away. I'm exhausted thinking about it, and so are many people in the civilized, red-eyed world.

And then, just when we are ready to call it quits rather than call it a day, we read Genesis 2:3. The great hope: "God blessed the seventh day and made it holy." Because God rested from all the work of days one through six, so can we.

At some point, we too have to learn to call it a day. But that involves trust, doesn't it? Trust that tomorrow will have enough minutes and hours for all of our to-dos. Trust that God's grace will be sufficient for our needs and wants and lists. Trust that sleep, actual real rest, is a valid way to call it a day. "It is night after long day," reads a long-ago prayer.

Today, what if we call it a day when the sun goes down, just like God did, and the new day begins right away with evening, with us trusting God. Put away the toolbox and the lists, and just trust. First there was evening, and then there was morning. Call it a day.

TRAVELING MERCY
Dear one,
Could you call it a day,
Beloved child?
Knowing that
I am both
The God of daytime
And the God of nighttime
And there will be plenty of day
Tomorrow?
Trust me.
Know that I have you covered
And designed you
To both trust me
And to rest.
It is night
After your very long day.
Please
Call it a day.

NOTE TO SELF
Why can't I call it a day?

CHRISTMAS IN THE DRUGSTORE

He was with God in the beginning. . . . In him was life,
and that life was the light of all mankind.

—JOHN 1:2, 4

I clicked the car fob and dashed into the nearby drugstore.[1]
We don't do Black Friday, that crazy desperation that has
come to kick off Christmas. But the day after Thanksgiving
is our traditional trip to check out the drugstore ads, especially
their buy-one-get-two-free wrapping paper deals. For years my
mom, sister, and I made the run. We added in children to the
trip as needed, and we always laughed our way through the
aisles, pushing the cart with its separate corners for each of our
purchases, sniffing fragrances, and buying stocking stuffers.

This year was different. With my mother in the hospital for
surgery, I barreled down to see her before Thanksgiving. The
holiday itself was a free-for-all, since we all live in different
towns and I live across state lines. It was the first Thanksgiving
Friday that we weren't together in years, and I swallowed my
heart back down out of my throat.

Inside the store, I checked my watch, grabbed my cell
phone, and called my sister. She picked up.

"Are you there?" I asked.

She rattled what sounded like a crisp advertising flier in the background. "Yes, in the entrance."

I knew that she was standing just inside the entrance of the drugstore in her hometown. This year, though we couldn't walk side by side down the aisle, we could still shop together. We perused our respective fliers and then started rolling.

"Are you at the candles?" she asked. (They were also buy one get two free, of course. We are nothing if not frugal.) "What do you think about the ocean breeze scent?"

I rummaged, lifted the lid on the jar, and coughed. "No, I didn't think so."

She sneezed. "Me neither."

"What about Dad's stocking? Any ideas?"

"How about these nuts?" A pause, shuffling and rearranging as the nuts went into her cart. We always get him nuts. He wouldn't be surprised at all, but he'd be pleased.

"Do you need any more wrapping paper?"

"I like this one with the blue in the background."

I dug through the tall tubes. "Oh, I like it too."

We wheeled our way around the stores, connected, but separate. I missed her dreadfully, and sometimes we choked up to be apart. Our cellular carrier dropped the call a couple times, but in the end, we got our shopping trip in. We didn't miss out on our tradition, though we sure missed our mom. We had Christmas, in the drugstore.

Creation was about connecting. Christmas is about connecting, about being together. Not just on earth's terms, with family reunions and presents under the tree and inhaling too much triple chocolate, heart-stopping fudge. Being together on heaven's terms. God longed to be with us—read that slowly, because it's the truth, and we don't even get it most of the time—but our hearts were so far away, so deadened by sin, so unable to keep the terms of the contract, broken in Eden. We couldn't be good enough to reach God. The connection was lousy on our end, the static of our sin always in the way. Our dropped calls and interruptions and dead zones stopped the relationship.

So instead, God did what we couldn't. He came to us in Christ, chose to connect with us in a way that would eradicate our past and all our inadequacies, and give us a lifeline. Christ ran that line straight to the door of our hearts.

"You there?" Christ asks. For God so loved the world. Enough to give us relationship with God and relationship with one another. A family that extends beyond our earthly ties. Christmas is God calling.

Christmas in the drugstore? It makes sense to me. God is, after all, the Great Physician.

TRAVELING MERCY
Dear one,
I am the Great Physician
And have been figuring out a way
To connect
Since dawn outside Eden.
Find your way
To me.
And I promise
I will find you.
In fact,
I already have.

NOTE TO SELF
All together now?

NOTE
1. A version of this devotion was printed as: Jane Rubietta, "Christmas in the Drugstore," *indeed* Magazine, November/December 2012, 4–5.

DECEMBER 22

LOOKING FOR EMMANUEL

"She will give birth to a son, and you are to give him the name
Jesus, because he will save his people from their sins."

—MATTHEW 1:21

Since Eden, we've been waiting for the One who would
walk among us as God did with Adam and Eve.[1] And now,
with Christmas coming, that time we remember the coming
of the One who would cancel the effects of the first couple's
first sin, my thoughts turn toward the grocery store.

In no way am I ready for Christmas, not in the commercial
sense. (Who has all their gifts purchased and wrapped? Cards
mailed? House decorated? Not I, certainly.) Nor in a spiritual
sense. The shelves of my soul-cupboard have been stripped
bare. Jesus might indeed have been coming, but my heart
feels like an empty can in the recycling bin. In the crunch of
the season and the press of life in general, I might not even
recognize God with us if I saw him.

The warehouse store parking lot was jammed. As I parked
and locked the door, a plea tore out from deep down: "I need
Emmanuel. Oh God, I need Emmanuel, God with us." I am
not beyond begging. Then I added a PS: "We also *really* need
some protein."

I wandered through the store, discouraged at the prices of everything, especially meat. "A *deal*, Lord," I reminded God. Just around the corner, a deep freezer case stood in the middle of the aisle, with a placard poking out like a yard-sale sign.

Peering inside, I exulted to see tons of frozen turkeys. "Ah ha! Left over from Thanksgiving. They should be on sale."

But the sign said a dollar and ninety cents a pound. "That is no deal, God, not with our economics." What was the store thinking? Then I looked more closely into the frost-lined bin. I had misplaced the decimal point. The sticker on the first turkey read, ".19."

What? Nineteen cents a *pound*? Turkey hasn't cost so little since 1930 has it? Could this be right? The other labels reported the same price. I loaded two twenty-three pound turkeys into the cavernous cart and pulled away. Then I thought again. We have a deep freeze. I turned back around and hefted four more.

The cart loaded with 140 pounds of frozen bird, I pushed along the aisle, beaming, practically riding the cart in my excitement. I told the next person I saw, "Turkeys! Can you believe it?" The customer peeled off to find the special, wheels leaving a rubber strip on the linoleum.

Down the next aisle, a woman stared at my bulging cart. Shoppers are savvy: "Those must be a deal if you have so many."

"Nineteen cents a pound!" I grinned. And then I got it. Isn't evangelism one beggar telling another where to find free bread?

My smile turned to a swelling of gratitude. Protein for the Rubiettas. For a long, long time.

We served turkey to our family and neighbors for six months. And every single time, I told the story. Emmanuel. God with us.

Jesus came. He flat-out showed up in a grocery store.

This year, I am watching with new eyes. You never know where Emmanuel will appear.

TRAVELING MERCY
Dear one,
I've been waiting
Since the beginning
To send my Son,
The One who would
Reign over life
And win out over death.
And now
He is here.
You'll find him
If you keep watching,
Keep loving,
Keep hoping.
And I hope you notice
We are loving you
Real big.

NOTE TO SELF
Keep watch. Spread the word.

NOTE
1. A version of this devotion was printed as: Jane Rubietta, "Looking for Emmanuel," *indeed* Magazine, November/December 2011, 54–55.

DECEMBER 23

CHRISTMAS LOVE SONG

But from everlasting to everlasting the LORD's love
is with those who fear him.

—PSALM 103:17

'Twas the season, supposedly.[1] Except, I was in no mood for decking the halls. My heart had gone missing, and the ache in its place throbbed incessantly.

How long since I'd felt love? How long since I'd experienced God's love in particular? Since Adam and Eve left Eden, maybe? While I inched my way through Saturday traffic on Chicago's North Side, made worse by people's last-minute holiday preparations, I could not remember the last love song from God. I tried to do all the right things: have quiet time, be silent for a few minutes daily, read the Scriptures, sing a hymn or two. But my heart was flat and the skin on my soul seemed exhausted and battered.

Coming straight from the hospital, where I'd camped for two nights on the floor beside a loved one's bed, with only an hour's straight sleep at a time, I'd sponge bathed and slapped some make-do makeup onto my quickly aging face. My eyes felt crusty and stared back in the mirror, red surrounding hazel. Perfect for the holidays.

The car in front of me delayed its jump from the starting line of a just-green signal, and I screamed in frustration as it missed the next light. "Drive, will you?" I didn't even look around to see if anyone noticed my road rage. I didn't care.

Pulling up to the following light, I groaned to see a man collecting for some Christmas charity. "Probably some hoax." Humbugging, I stared in the opposite direction. I didn't want to drop meter money into his little coffee can.

But the Will-Smith-looking gentleman approached my window, an engaging smile on his face. I lifted my hands in a move meant to show destitution. He grinned some more and made a roll-down-your-window motion with his free hand.

What could it hurt to crank down the window a few inches? I complied, and immediately he gave a small whistle.

"You are the best-looking thing I've seen in my life. I cannot take my eyes off you. And we're collecting for needy children in Chicago—we'll feed five hundred kids on Christmas day."

A real hard sell, I dug through my purse, couldn't find my wallet, and couldn't find money in the door rests.

"That's OK, Miss Diamond," he said, spotting my fake glittery earrings. "Whew-hew! Looking at you is eeee-nough."

"You're nuts." I laughed at him and kept hunting for coins. "My husband doesn't keep change in his ashtray, I guess."

"Your husband is one lucky man. I pray for someone like you in my life every single day."

Horns honked behind me as the light turned green. I found twelve cents and stuffed them in the slot, smiled at him, and drove forward.

A few blocks later, I laughed at his words. He sure had his patter down. Then, at another red light, I began to cry. Not because I missed the green. Because I finally saw the lengths God had to go to get to my sore, sad heart.

"Did you hear what he said, that man with the coin can? Did you hear *my* words back there? You are the most beautiful woman in the world to me, and I am one lucky God to have you. *Miss Diamond*."

And in the man's smile, and in his words, I recognized the long-term delight and love song of God, right there at a red light in Chicago.

Sometimes, I guess we just have to stop.

TRAVELING MERCY
Dear one,
Everlasting—
That's the kind of love
Available since the beginning
Of the beginning.
I hope you'll stop.
I hope you'll listen.
I hope you'll believe me.
I hope you'll sing along.

NOTE TO SELF
Listen. Join the song.

NOTE
1. A version of this devotion was printed as: Jane Rubietta, "Christmas Love Song," *indeed* Magazine, November/December 2010, 55–56.

DECEMBER 24

SETTLING IN

For as in Adam all die, so in Christ all will be made alive.

—1 Corinthians 15:22

Utility trucks trundled up and workers disembarked from inside perches. Boxes were slit open as extension ladders rattled up alongside the house across the street. Time for Christmas in our new neighborhood. Now, lights blanket houses and trees with perfectly straight, perfectly spaced Christmas cheer and order. Nary a bulb absent from the displays, no rogue blinking, all perfectly timed to turn on and off at appropriate hours. Everything just perfect.

In keeping with the season and with the Joneses, I've left some shriveled gourds on the small porch of our quaint little home. At least I managed to scrape the frozen pumpkins off the steps and throw the bowling-ball type orbs into the garbage. The gourds are a holdout for me, a resistance of the obligatory holiday schedule and perfect appearance.

On some levels our recent move has been difficult. With an overwhelming workload, we couldn't finish unpacking, settling, and crafting a home from the old walls. The kitchen, bathrooms, and main bedroom are serviceable but not homey.

We gave away the sofas, so home isn't particularly comfortable. Our sitting options are dining room chairs (of which we seem to have several large sets yet only two people in the place) and two wooden, straight-backed rocking chairs. Sort of his-and-hers.

With the unsettledness of our home, my life also feels unsettled. We've managed, though, to live in this state for months.

It's Christmas that bothers me. In addition to not being arranged, the house isn't even clean, let alone decorated. I feel a vague shame about that, because if I just had more energy or just slept less I could be more ready. Christmas tasks back up in train-wreck effect, waiting for me to tick them off.

In a larger sense, though, this has been good for me. Not unpacking and not settling have forced me to detach from the typical trappings of the season—the tree, the lights, the warmly decorated home, the menu plan, the Christmas music, the hot chocolate, and the ingredients for fresh pumpkin cranberry bread.

Instead, I escape for my office and spend time with Emmanuel, God with us. I read the lectionary Scriptures for the day, wait, and pray. Sometimes I sing an Advent hymn, such as, "O Come, O Come Emmanuel." Sometimes I walk and just try to point my heart toward God.

As I consider Adam and Eve, excluded from Eden and then bereft of God's presence, I am all the more grateful for the grace God sent. This season, without the decorations in place or even the furniture to place them on, has felt more homelike than ever as I strive to live in the middle of the coming of Christ. To understand the implications of Christ's initial advent.

To watch for his coming in my daily life and in this world. And to realize that I am one of the ways Christ comes into this world now. Christ makes a way through my attitude, my love, and even my eye contact with another. He comes through me noticing people, not taking myself so seriously, and not getting anxious about my time-poverty so I can pay attention to others instead. I remind myself to be kind and that people have hard days and hard lives and we would understand if we could see into their story. A new slant on settling in.

TRAVELING MERCY

Dear one,
You've looked for home
Since leaving Eden,
Now your home is in me
And in my Christ,
The Promised One.
And though you feel unsettled
And unnoticed,
I am paying attention to you
And to your longings
This season.
I know your story,
And I can see around the bend.
You are finding your way
Home.

NOTE TO SELF

How does Christ come through me?

DECEMBER 25

PAST IMPERFECT

The Lord God made all kinds of trees grow out of the ground.

—Genesis 2:9

"Mom, could we please just set a date for getting our tree this year?" our son asked.[1] The date for Christmas tree shopping is always after he gets home from college, somewhere around December 20. But when he rolled home on December 23 to a hole where a tree should dominate with its pine scent and towering green, he motored me straight out the door for the tree store.

Turns out, the trees available two days before Christmas consist of millions of loose needles that you need to glue to a dowel rod. Build-a-tree. Who knew? We chose one of the three un-Edenic trees left in the entire lot and could've walked home with it under one arm, it was so light. Our tree criteria this year whittled down to one stipulation: the tree must be taller than we are. Only one tree qualified.

We propped it in a pot of water in the shed, slit the net casing, and returned a few hours later to check its acclimation and relaxation. There wasn't much difference between binding and relaxing for this poor tree, the homeliest wallflower (walltree) on the planet, the last one picked at the Christmas dance.

In the family room, the tree stood near the window like a hairy lamppost, straight-laced and narrow, filling only two feet of the room. A twenty-four-inch appendage, like a spare arm, tucked tight around its neighbors, as though the branch was trying to blend in. We laughed until I doubled over, and Josh rolled on the floor. We didn't even set up the tree stand right—one red metal leg was jammed into the base at an angle and tilted the entire tree.

The memory of that healing laughter bolstered us as we gathered at the dinner table before the Christmas Eve service. Our numbers had shrunk to three that year. Missing family members and painful stories shared around the meal made swallowing difficult and left holes in the fabric of the evening. We grieved, and regret stuck in our throats. The candlelight emphasized our own wavering shadows.

Christmas is a time of remembering, and remembering isn't always happy. Most family stories are like our homely Christmas tree: a make-do tree, with its strange asymmetry, poor balance, and crooked stance in its stand. But the scent of a family, like the pine and the sap and the outdoors coming in? That scent somehow creates a wholeness of imperfection, love, tolerance, and forgiveness.

As we left the table that night, the words "O come, O come Emmanuel, and ransom captive Israel" sighed through my soul. The next morning, I grieved for the captivity of this world, the brokenness, and then relaxed into the truth of Christmas: the Christ, the God with us, who came into the sharp fragments of our brokenness.

On a deep breath, I opened the Scriptures to the morning's reading, Isaiah 51 and came to verse 11: "Those the LORD has rescued will return. They will enter Zion with singing; everlasting joy will crown their heads. Gladness and joy will overtake them, and sorrow and sighing will flee away."

Christmas present. For all of us, families near and families far, filled with grief and laughter and imperfection redolent as fresh-cut pine. Gladness and joy and singing. And hope. Hope of Christmas future—Christmas perfect.

TRAVELING MERCY

Dear one,
Evergreen
My hope for you,
My plans for my loved ones.
Christ with you forevermore;
The Tree of Life
Ever ready.
Until that day,
Practice your gladness and joy,
Your hope,
In the middle of the imperfects.
The day is coming
When sorrow flees.
It's been a long wait.
But I promise
Christ is coming back.

NOTE TO SELF

Finding evergreen. Sing.

NOTE

1. A version of this devotion was printed as: Jane Rubietta, "Past Imperfect," *indeed* Magazine, November/December 2013, 3–4.

HANDS-ON

Then the LORD God formed a man from the dust of the ground.

—GENESIS 2:7

For those first six days of creation, "God said" and it was so. God spoke it all into being with powerful, creative words. But in the almost last act on the last day of forming this wildly varied and rich world, God packed together some dirt and shaped the first man. Possibly *adamah*, in the Hebrew. Dirt. The dirt man made history, and eventually adamah became Adam. His wife would give new meaning to the term "coming alongside" as God handmade her from one of Adam's ribs.

This personal touch would forever distinguish God's relationship with people. God the sculptor, whose first and second human creations bore the marks of God's creative genius, of perfection, and of the indelible stamp of "miracle."

The cells, systems, circulation, organs—eyes that would see and respond. A brain entirely dependent on the other systems in place, but capable of carrying thought, making wise decisions, and interacting with others, including God. Skin, soft to touch, essential for protecting all those insides from germs and harm. The list rolls on and on. I couldn't begin to describe all the interconnectedness of one single human being with all the elements that must function correctly to allow an eye to blink or a fingernail to grow.

This one creation, adamah, led to billions of unique compositions throughout the centuries. No one would carry the same DNA, have exactly the same personality, proclivities, gifts, hopes, or dreams.

Just wait with the sheer brilliance of this moment.

That miracle is about you. About me. For all the years of feeling inadequate, under-efficient, or somehow defective, let that sink in. You are a miracle. For the years of low self-esteem and the damage done by others to contribute to that sense of worthlessness, hear this: You are a miracle.

And then we get it. The rest of creation, God said, would be "after its own kind," but this *pièce de résistance* of creation? After God's likeness, in God's image. "Let us make mankind in our image, in our likeness," God said (Gen. 1:26).

We have trivialized the miracle of human beings. Each of us handcrafted by the God of the universe. Though perhaps we don't reflect that Artist much in daily life, the imprint of God's work carries through to every single baby ever born.

Walking miracles, one-of-a-kind artistic expressions of the God who has no equal, the one true God.

And as for those who have told you otherwise, who have accused you, abused you, demeaned you, wounded you, declared you worthless—it is all a lie. A blatant, boldfaced lie. If others' hands have hurt you, do not allow their wounds to win. Return to the hands of God, who loved you since before forever and whose hands will always hold you gently.

Frail and fragile flesh and blood though you be. Fallible as all get-out. Imperfect, quite capable of sin, of hurting others, of doing damage. But still—handmade by the very One who created this astounding world and galaxy. Handcrafted by the God of the universe. Made malleable in heart, able to be molded and shaped into God's image more and more.

You are branded, friend. Made by God. Believe that today.

TRAVELING MERCY

Dear one,
Your wounds at others' hands
Were not from me.
You are shaped,
Loved
From the beginning,
Branded with my mark,
One of a kind,
A designer original.
Listen, sweet one,
You are the person
I dreamed of,
A flat-out
Flesh and blood
Miracle.

NOTE TO SELF

How do I live like the miracle that I am?

LIFE-BREATHED

[God] breathed into [the man's] nostrils the breath of life,
and the man became a living being.

—GENESIS 2:7

Sledding in the winter left me gasping and wheezing but refusing to miss out on the unfettered joy and hilarity of child's play in the snow. When swimming more than half a lap of the pool, I thought my lungs would explode, as though I'd been submerged underwater like a free diver with no training. Or like someone had forgotten the gills. For me, asthma is like trying to breathe through wet sand or mud. In an attack, the filter never opens to allow a full breath.

Sometimes I awakened in the dead of night, the filter closing off my air passage. I sprang from bed and ran gasping and panicked into the hallway to find my parents. Years later, when my husband and I lived in the country across from a grain elevator, my breathing problems kicked into attack mode, and doctors finally listened and prescribed an inhaler. When I breathed from an inhaler in the dark of night and drew my first midnight-deep breath, I felt like I'd discovered outer space, as though I'd evacuated the confines of our home and lifted above the sky and could *feel* the whole Milky Way. Like the galaxy lived within my lungs. I had never felt so free, so unencumbered, as that night.

Oxygen is more than a little bit important. With too-low levels of oxygen, our hearts over-function, trying to pump the scant reserves through the bloodstream. Oxygen-deprived muscles may cramp and seize. Of course, without oxygen for very long our brains sustain damage, and ultimately we die. Turns out, it's hard to find your way without oxygen.

The system God set in place from the very beginning is brilliant. We will always be oxygen dependent, unable to depart for long without the right amount of O_2. It is true for our physical bodies and true for our spiritual selves as well. The term used in Genesis 2:7, "breath of life," means "breath or blast of breath; and by extension life, life force, spirit."[1] Without that blast of breath from God, that life force, that spirit-breathed air, we cannot sustain spiritual life.

I try this, now, at my desk. The day has been a mixture of encouragement and discouragement, and maybe the tiniest element of sleep deprivation. When I am tired, my spine curls into a C-shape and I don't breathe deeply. Now, I inhale until my rib cage expands and imagine fresh God-breathed air filling me, sending oxygen coursing through my bloodstream and my brain. When filled with breath, my posture improves, as does my energy level. When I focus on God and invite the Holy Spirit to breathe into me, I find that my soul-levels of life expand.

Just as in the beginning, God, blasting breath into us, fills us with hope, with power, with all we need to sustain the spiritual life and function in this world. No more O_2 deprivation. No more Spirit deprivation.

TRAVELING MERCY
Dear one,
Breathe in
My presence.
Invite my Spirit
To fill you and refill you
Throughout your day,
And you will live
Not on your limited air
But on my unlimited resources
Of life.
Breathe in
Again and again.
I will sustain
You.

NOTE TO SELF
Breathe in me, breath of God.

NOTE
1. *The Strongest NIV Exhaustive Concordance* (Grand Rapids, MI: Zondervan, 1999), 1456, #5972.

SOUL SPEAK

A river watering the garden flowed from Eden;
from there it was separated into four headwaters.

—GENESIS 2:10

Ranchers and farmers look for land with water running through it. Water means life for livestock, plants, and people. Citizens fight over water rights; land contracts include specific details about who can take water from what ditch. In some areas, guns are permitted to resolve questions and disputes over water rights.

The rivers that bracketed the garden of Eden remind us of the life-saving and life-giving presence of water. They speak of boundaries, natural barriers in the land. And they trigger a longing for something just beyond our reach, now, as we look backward to the world's beginning.

The sun bracketed a recent day, presiding over the Ohio River at dawn and sunset. I stood at the bank, entranced by the endlessly moving water and the light pouring into it and transforming it into a running molten stream. In the brilliance, any debris disappeared and only loveliness remained. I filled the lungs of my soul, breathing deeply of the scent of river water and warm sun. The hues of red and orange and yellow turned the world ambient and welcoming. It pulsed with benediction.

I breathed in the glowing. And I wept.

The principles of relationship, beauty, space, creativity, and refilling shine in our Book of beginning. That God cared enough to plant a garden and then to plant us in that garden — isn't beauty essential to our mental health? How incalculable the cost to people who live in ugliness. Living without beauty wreaks a violence on our souls. Eden issues a clear statement: We were created for beauty.

No doubt that's one of the reasons that places of punishment seem brutal in form and function. Not only do we not want anyone to be comfortable — in a supposed place of penitence, the more austere the better, no distractions to stop the repenting — but do we also want to keep them oppressed? Life without beauty is a form of oppression.

Whether imprisoned by the penal institution or by psychological pain, whether oppressed by seemingly insignificant work or overwhelming responsibilities, we are desperate for the soul-expansion beauty brings. We are so rest-deprived that an entire industry of sleep aids offers us hope for sale. Because rest from the insanity is a large hope on our wish list.

God's rhythm of night and day initiates this principle of creative refillment. Night after long day and day after restful night reestablishes our vision. We lose our way in the austerity of a long workweek filled with much that is not lovely, much that is outright ugly. A day of rest is one way that God established to help us find beauty in our surroundings, in our God, and yes, even in ourselves.

I've never been legalistic about a day of rest; there is nothing traditional about a ministry workweek except that it is long and Sundays are not a day off. But somewhere, somehow, we must find refilling stations. Pockets of time where God pours into us and speaks the language we each hear and understand best. Even small moments of noticing.

Adam and Eve could hear the sound of the Lord God in the garden. How do we hear God's voice? Maybe it's a waterfall. A worship song. A bell choir. A sermon. A jog in the winter-brisk air. A sweet two-year-old singing the Johnny Appleseed blessing did it for me today. I cried and praised God and prayed in a new way. And then, returned to my day.

TRAVELING MERCY

Dear one,
The rivers form boundaries.
And your time with me
And my time with you
Create a boundary of replenishment,
A place to rest.
Hope isn't for sale.
It's a costly gift,
But free to you.
So come;
I speak your heart's language.

NOTE TO SELF

Discover heart language; listen in; speak it often.

NOT GOOD TO BE ALONE

"It's not good for the Man to be alone; I'll make him
a helper, a companion."

—GENESIS 2:18 MSG

Andrew jumped at the poke in the back that first day of psych class during his sophomore year of high school. At first, he couldn't identify the sensation. He twisted around to see the bright-smiling girl who had just jabbed him with her pen, upper body draped over her desk. She chirped, "Hey! Weren't we in a class together last year?"

Fast forward ten years: Andrew and Lizzie face each other on the ninety-ninth floor of the Willis Tower sky deck, surrounded by family and friends, and declare their commitment through heartfelt marriage vows.

The minister invites all assembled to bow in prayer for this couple. He cites the famous verse that rings so true on this night, "It is not good for the man to be alone" (Gen. 2:18). Nor a woman for that matter. Nor anyone, actually. But the pastor doesn't say all that.

Little did Adam know how much better his future would be with the helpmate God would handcraft. So much easier to shell nuts, forage for supper, till the ground, and pound the grain with a partner. But there were many more reasons to be revealed, for Adam and Eve and for Andrew and Lizzie.

Why all of this additional goodness from God? Why isn't it good for anyone to be alone too long?

Five years into their platonic friendship, Andrew popped a question to Lizzie at a bookstore: "Will you be my girlfriend? My one and only?" Within a short time, both of their worlds turn upside down with life's calamities, including each of them losing a parent. First, Andrew became Lizzie's helpmate as she sank into what seemed like an endless sadness. Then, Lizzie gripped Andrew's hand so he wouldn't completely disappear into a deep quagmire of depression. During that time, it was as if Lizzie was bone of Andrew's bone and they were one.

The word *helpmate* carries the idea of completion of one another. Not just the woman completing the man, as some interpret it. Rather, the word is a round-trip experience, each shoring up the other's weaknesses and needs, filling in the other's gaps and gifts. Carrying each other's load.

Imagine down the road, how devastating for Adam to lose one son at the hand of another. Perhaps Adam was reminded of the voice during the times he and Eve embraced in the wake of Abel's death. "It is not good to be alone, so I will make you a helpmate." Married or single, we eventually need the embrace and support of another, whether through platonic or romantic companionship.

One implication of God's ominous and gracious statement is the recognition that none of us ought to be independent of others, "a rock, an island," as Simon and Garfunkel wrote. To be alone increases vulnerability.

You may be unhappily married, unequally yoked, single and happy or unhappy, but this word from God is true. "It is not good to be alone." And the promise holds forth: God has created helpmates for us if we will look around.

We all encounter pain in this world. It is not good for a man or woman to be alone, because helpmates can lift us when we fall, correct us when we stray, and sit with us when there is nothing to say.

TRAVELING MERCY
Dear one,
It is not good to be alone.
You need someone to catch you
When you fall,
Not if you fall,
To hold you in your fear,
Challenge you in your sin,
Help you find your way.
Find your companions,
Friends or family,
Your helpmates.
It's much better
To do life
Together.
You, me, and another
Makes we.

NOTE TO SELF
Better together.

LEAVING HOME, FINDING HOME

That is why a man leaves his father and mother and is united to his wife, and they become one flesh.

—GENESIS 2:24

Meet Mack, age 36. His mom still washed his clothes and cooked his meals without charging him a dime to live at home. Mom truly loved him, and Mack loved being loved, but was this helping him grow up into a man that God uses?

Since it is not good for anyone to be alone, it seems that God wants all of us to find partners in this world, true helpmates. To this end, Genesis 2:24 says we have to eventually leave home. As a trapeze artist will attest, it takes faith to let go of the familiar and live in limbo, holding onto nothing and then hopefully grasping the solid handle of a new swing. It's hard to leave, hard to find a new home, and perhaps even harder to be stuck in between, all alone. But we must leap.

At 32, Diana knew how to make a home but she was not learning how to relate to other people. It's not clear if she was socially delayed because she still lived with her parents, or if she stayed at home because of her awkwardness around others. Could verse 24 be hinting that we will stagnate if we depend on our parents indefinitely?

To leave home and still maintain a connection to the community we left while we form a new one is challenging. Still, the two communities need not be mutually exclusive.

Perhaps a secret to growing up is figuring out how to simultaneously cherish the best of previous relationships while leaving behind the tempting patterns. Home may have been our haven, but also a place where unhealthy denial and destructive patterns kept us from healing and growing up in Christ.

Pamela blamed her parents for her eating disorder. Her dad numbed his pain with food, and her mom under-ate to compensate financially in their growing family. Both patterns created isolation instead of community. So Pamela developed a debilitating dance of death with food. Clinging to food made bonding with others, in new and healthy relationships, impossible.

More than once, Jake's parents asked, "How will you make a living as an actor? Do you want to be a starving artist?" But God created Jake to be an artist. Jake had to leave those statements behind. Perhaps the leaving entails making a clean break from any parts of past relationships that hold us back and bond us to anything but God and God's future for us.

Though Jasmine's parents and grandparents mirrored God's love, there had been conflict and damage. On the precipice of leaving and cleaving, she created a ritual to help build a bridge from one home to the next. Instead of a traditional moment of silence at her wedding, we remembered how those elders had modeled Christ's love, then with prayers of thanksgiving we blew bubbles skyward.

If God intends that we find helpmates to create life-giving community, we must detach from unhealthy parts of past relationships, without losing the best parts of ourselves *or* those relationships. We find our way in leaving, whether to marriage or supportive friendships, and we cleave to God who formed us. Leaving allows us, then, to become the best version of ourselves. And frees us for relationship with others.

TRAVELING MERCY
Dear one,
Leave your past
And cleave to me.
Healing happens
In positive community,
And you'll become
Who you're designed to be.
It's a win-win
For you,
For the people in your past,
For your future,
And for the world.

NOTE TO SELF
What patterns do I leave? To whom do I cleave?

FROM BREATH TO BLESSED

And God blessed the seventh day, and made it holy.

—GENESIS 2:3

On the seventh day, God rested, establishing a rhythm of work and rest that would continue through time and centuries until this minute. Rest, essential for revitalization, allows us breathing space, room to downshift from the panic-driven lifestyle so many of us embrace.

With increasing diagnoses of adrenal exhaustion, kicking back from technology and stimulation helps repair our adrenal function. And that's not even actual sleep we're talking about; that's a sort of deactivating that actually rejuvenates. Ah, but sleep—sleep, sweet sleep—critical for brain function and for immune rebuilding. Even for weight control and weight loss, they're discovering. For cell repair and regeneration. Some people tell me that their bed is their favorite place in the house, a haven from the sheer volume and velocity of their lives.

When God rested, the word in the Hebrew used for that rest means "ceased": God ceased from the work of creation. Whether we cease from our labors by sleeping long enough to be restored or by repairing creatively, we are invited into a resting place.

If we don't have space or breathing room, we experience compromised health, relationships, and job performance. Without space, we overreact to stimuli. We get our feelings hurt more easily; our boundaries either crumble or become rigid and demanding. Perfectionism tightens its grip. Maybe it looks like not trying because we can't measure up to our own standards, or it may look like expecting even more of ourselves and others. We slip easily into anger rather than resolution. We are restless and in our restlessness we harm ourselves and others.

And without adequate sleep, our subconscious minds never get to the dream state, where we work through problems that arise during our too-many minutes of being awake. We stop dreaming, literally, and too often cease to dream about God's best for us, about using our gifts. We stop imagining how to find our way or what being fruitful looks like. Multiplying? Forget about it. There's just not enough of us to stretch any further.

But rest is the antidote to all that.

What if we redefine a day of rest, and rather than mandating it for a twenty-four-hour period, we start small? If rest looked like space on a daily basis, how could you bring breathing room into your life? Something beyond the overused term, "quiet time." What work could you resist doing, for a few minutes, in order to rest in God's presence?

Perhaps it's just breathing. Practice that with me. (I bet you do this fairly often, this breathing business. But humor me.) Pull up all the anxiety you carry within you. Now, exhale it all, focusing on God and clearing both your lungs and your soul. Breathe in, deliberately, a characteristic of God. Breathe out your pain. Breathe in God's comfort. Breathe out your fear. Breathe in God's promise to never leave you.

Breathe out, breathe in. And the rest from God fills us, expanding our lungs and coursing into our bloodstream and brain. Rest.

What a marvelous plan. A miracle. It is good for all that ails us.

TRAVELING MERCY
Dear one,
You work so hard.
You work so long,
And I would love
To see you take a load off,
Literally,
But also spiritually.
Let go of your need to earn your keep
And simply trust me
For a few minutes,
Or a lot of minutes,
This day.
Allow me to breathe into you
As I breathed life into Adam and Eve.
You are breath-deprived,
And I would love to help you
Catch your breath
Today.

NOTE TO SELF
Catch my breath, and catch up with God.

JANUARY DEVOTIONS

THE GREAT UNKNOWN

See, I am doing a new thing! Now it springs up;
do you not perceive it? I am making a way in
the desert. And streams in the wasteland.

—Isaiah 43:19

January 1. New day, new year. We stand at the portal of a batch of 365 big unknowns; 8,760 hours still in the mint and not in our pockets to jingle like coins. It's like looking into the mouth of a safe, a vault full of unspent minutes, unexperienced moments. The future awaits. We celebrate, blow party screamers, shoot fireworks, and cheer when the clock strikes midnight, and we shout "Happy New Year!"

But truly, we know not what we cheer, what we celebrate, not really. The New Year's seconds are still un-ticked, its minutes tightly wound, its days tucked into a calendar known only to God. Our clocks and computers and phones may automatically transition into this New Year, but we may not.

We try. We make resolutions. "This year, I will . . ." and we fill in the blanks. Work harder, work smarter, change jobs, love the family more or better or differently, sleep more (or less!), lose weight, exercise, gut my entire life and get a makeover. We have changes we'll make. We'll shoot for being better at everything. This year we will make it happen.

It's not the most realistic approach to a new year, deciding to revamp every aspect of our lives. Plus, we have a history of failed performances, of blowing some new resolutions by day one. By day thirty, we've scrapped most of them. By day 365, they're totally the stuff of journals and logs, long forgotten. (Until we resurrect them on the new January 1.)

Not forgotten are the difficulties of the previous year. Not only were we not who we'd hoped, but life wasn't what we'd hoped. The year unveiled unexpected changes. Changes in the economy, both our personal economy and the world's. Changes in our relationships, jobs, health, dreams, and spiritual journey. Changes we didn't know to prepare for. It doesn't feel like freedom, all these unexpecteds.

And then, there are those changes that we expected, perhaps even instigated. Maybe we looked for a new job or promotion and got it, and the going has been harder than we figured. Maybe we found a new house, on purpose, and though good it's meant even more change. What we thought offered more freedom, instead amped up anxiety.

The New Year highlights change, and changes, good and bad, take a toll on our soul. They cost us, much more than pennies in our pockets. If it were pennies, we could "find a penny, pick it up, and all the day we'll have good luck." No, these changes are not about finding good luck to make it through, spare change to drop into the vending machine at the edge of the path. They cost us emotionally, physically, and relationally. They arrive at our door like creditors, demanding payment that we do not have, resources not at our disposal.

New Year's Day is a day of transition, and transition, by definition, means passage, movement. Here, in the land of change, we will not stay. We will pass through. Day by day by day. And eventually, we'll find our way, travel-weary, sun-burned, but alive. So hold tight. There is a way through. You may spend all your pennies of time and energy, but your journey will not expend you.

TRAVELING MERCY
Dear one,
You look ahead and see
Unfamiliar terrain.
Unchosen problems.
Unsought change.
But you know me.
I am doing a new work,
In you and in your world
This year.
As you stand on this threshold
To the unknown,
Take my hand.
I know the way
And will lead you
To the Promised Land.

NOTE TO SELF
God knows my unknowns.

JANUARY 2

COVERED

The man and his wife were both naked,
but they were not ashamed.

—Genesis 2:25 net

How do you stand naked in front of someone for the first time without having some feelings about that? Most people would love a better-looking body double for the naked times in their lives.

Naked and not ashamed. What a statement of wholeness and safety. The word *naked* implies integrity or innocence, a lack of fear. No sense of exploitation. "[They] were both naked, but they were not ashamed" reminds us that if all is well between us and others, between us and God, and between us and ourselves, there will be no shame.

Maybe with a rough draft of chapter 3 in mind, the writer of Genesis knew that shame was coming. Shame would enter the garden and haunt the human heart forever. We would find it forever difficult to hear and believe God's "very good" statement about us.

Being naked is about being vulnerable. And vulnerable is scary. Who of us is comfortable when other people see our belly, especially in winter? Or our flabby emotional attitudes?

But, if Adam and Eve are to be helpmates, not just fellow hunters and gatherers, vulnerability needs to extend to all areas of relationship, every kind of intercourse. Without vulnerability, we can't pray together, talk honestly, learn from mistakes, and grow into God's likeness.

During her single daughter's holiday visit, a mother feels the daughter overstepped the bounds of hospitality. Her adult child thinks hospitality should have fewer expectations. As they try to unravel it, shame threatens to push them apart, neither of them feeling safe enough to backtrack and be vulnerable with the other. Shame makes it almost impossible to feel safe enough to own your inadequacies and say, "I am sorry."

Then when we do, shame is like tar that clings to the underbelly of our car after we drive through a freshly asphalted construction zone. It threatens to stick to us forever as that residual feeling of worthlessness lingers long after we've admitted guilt and been forgiven.

Because of shame, we wonder, how we can possibly be together with others *without* hiding behind flimsy fig leaves of pride and invincibility and pretension. So shame is the enemy of vulnerability and therefore intimacy. And without intimacy, we might as well be alone. But God can wash that tar-like shame away, if we will allow it. And we must if we are to live in healthy relationship.

A group of pastors gathers to ask each other only one question: "How is it with your soul?" *à la* John Wesley's Oxford small group meetings. In gatherings of professionals, it's tempting to convince the others that you're worthy of their esteem — but how can you brag about your soul? Wesley's question scraped away the skin of pride and reached the core: We are all afraid and love-starved. Talking about this takes trust in each other and in God's covering of us.

We can learn to be emotionally and spiritually vulnerable. The gift of shamelessness in Eden can be recovered in our grace-filled relationships with God and others. Grace is, after all, undeserved favor, unmerited assistance.

If there is grace, Leanne can hold up an emotional mirror to Robert and show him how he looks. She can share how his behavior feels to her. If there is grace, Robert may hear God's voice speaking to him, through his helpmate. Whether with friends or family or fellow professionals, if we can feel safe enough to be emotionally naked, we can learn from any human failure.

Shame. The opposite of God's "very good." Today, may we receive God's covering in all our vulnerabilities. Grace given. Grace received. We'll find our way, covered. With grace.

TRAVELING MERCY
Dear one,
· My "Very good"
Still covers you,
Though it's hard for you to hear
And believe and share.
For today
Know that I see you naked
To the core,
And I still say
"Very good."
My words
Are all the covering you need
To live and love
In this world
And with me.

NOTE TO SELF
What covers me? How do I cover others?

JANUARY 3

VOICES

Now the serpent was more crafty than any of the
wild animals that the LORD God had made.

—GENESIS 3:1

Delighted. Delightful. Free. Safe. Alive. These words and
many more describe the state of Adam and Eve when Genesis
says, "The man and his wife were both naked, but they were
not ashamed" (Gen. 2:25 NET). They experienced no worries
about exploitation, no hindrances, no sense of vulnerability,
no feelings of corruption, no doubt, no negative anything.
According to the NET Bible, *nakedness* in this verse conveys
a lack of fear and a sense of either innocence or integrity.

Given the order of the Scriptures, this shouldn't surprise us.
The man and woman were naked, unashamed, free, innocent,
and full of integrity (which means "wholeness") at the end
of chapter 2. Yes, yes, yes. All that glory 'round about. And
then, Genesis 3:1: "Now the serpent . . ."

What a cleverly devised attack on this first couple, finding
the one weak chink in their armor of innocence. If the husband
and wife had ever heard another voice besides God's, we don't
see it in the Scriptures. If anything else speaks in this new
creation, we don't hear it.

And the serpent's voice sounded louder and certainly more current than the other voice they'd heard, the voice of God, their creator. The new voice sowed doubt where none existed before, replacing the voice in their souls and in their eardrums.

The serpent seized the advantage with this new couple in their naïveté, their in-exposure to anything other than goodness. He took advantage of their nakedness, their entire lack of shame, and their trusting nature. Three sentences from the serpent and the couple capitulated.

"Did God really say, 'You must not eat from any tree in the garden'?" (Gen. 3:1). (Obviously God didn't say that. What would they eat for fruit then? But temptation is not rational.)

"You will not certainly die," the vile one said (Gen. 3:4). (Blatant lie. Make God look like a liar. They wouldn't die immediately, true, but they definitely wouldn't live forever, not physically.) "For God knows that when you eat from it your eyes will open and you will be like divine beings who know good and evil" (Gen. 3:5 NET). (This may be the only almost-truth in this entire dialogue.)

Oh, the appeal of that wisdom, that understanding. Adam and Eve listened to this most recent voice echoing in their ears, tempted beyond all reason to reach for the fruit from that tree, to taste and see.

They listened, they took, and they tasted. Then they saw. With opened eyes, they saw their own nakedness, saw it with newly attached shame, an unfurling of horror and separation.

Was there weeping in the garden at this defiling? Did the glory of the whole world around them suddenly dull, or was that dimming just the veil that slid so smoothly over their just-opened eyes? And would they forevermore wish they'd memorized the sound of God's voice and learned the nuances of love and provision they heard every time God had spoken?

So when Jesus said, many centuries later, "My sheep listen to my voice; I know them, and they follow me. . . . No one will snatch them out of my hand" (John 10:27–28), maybe the Jews in the audience harkened back to Eden. To the first couple, listening to the wrong voice.

May we be like sheep, listening to our creator Shepherd's voice, recognizing and following it above all the lure and lore and voices in this world.

TRAVELING MERCY
Dear one,
Do not let your armor's chink
Cause an ear deaf to my voice,
Leaving you unhearing of my love for you,
My longing for you,
The best I have to offer you.
Taste and see
That I am good
And my word is sweeter
Than the honey
And the honeycomb.

NOTE TO SELF
Filling up with God's words leaves no room for lies.

MASS COMMUNICATION

"You will not certainly die," the serpent said to the woman.

—GENESIS 3:4

While I perched on an uncomfortable bench inside the cell phone provider's store, waiting and waiting, the room buzzed and vibrated. Oversized televisions overstimulated the entire atmosphere. I called my husband to rescue me. His own noisy surroundings muffled his ringtone. He couldn't hear the phone. Frustrated and ambushed, I focused on the multiple screens around the shop.

People send 3.7 billion texts per day. Really?

So many attempts at communicating. Imagine all those messages, all entirely devoid of inflection, of tone. (And imagine how many of them with Englext, my term for shorthand spelling in texts.) And all of those attempts to communicate, some profound, some banal, but all of them attempts. How often were they received and appreciated, or even understood in terms of the emotional meaning behind them? Or misunderstood and misinterpreted?

Then imagine, once upon a time, when a triune God decided to communicate out of an overflowing heart, all the love and longing and beauty possible. And those words that spoke that universe into existence, that one-of-a-kind masterpiece of composition.

And imagine how quickly the message was misinterpreted: "Surely God didn't mean you would die! Surely you deserve the very thing that has been withheld from you. Surely God isn't really good, because God knows that the second you eat this scrumptious, luscious, unimaginable fruit, you will become like him."

So many voices compete for God's voice, so many choice fruits vie for God's presence in our world and our lives. So many lies hiss into our souls, a visual and verbal cacophony.

On my bench, trying to avoid eye contact with those big-screen TVs, I began to understand the tiniest pixel—maybe the single message we need to decipher from these oversized hieroglyphics of sight and sound bombarding us.

We want to matter.

But we look around; we want that screen or phone or house or job or spouse. We want, we want. And this, too, is part of finding our way. We have a God-given heart created for desire—and desire makes us feel special, or at least makes us want to feel special. But it's nearly impossible to hear the emotion whispered under the words screamed by the world. The words and world promise delectable fulfillment and meaning, but instead drive us to distraction on the way to bondage. We compulsively check our devices for communications. Did someone try to reach me? Am I important this very second? Does someone love me?

Hear, then, the good news: God has been writing notes, giving presents, and sending pictures day after day.

We want to matter. We do matter. We matter to God. If we didn't matter, the world would never have been spoken into creation. That's the entire message behind the words of creation.

It's the oldest song in the book, really.

God.

Loves.

Us.

Maybe today we can hear the inflection in the voices around us, beckoning and wooing us down the wrong path. Maybe we can hear the words, spoken throughout thousands of years, in so many ways . . . more than the 3.7 billion texts sent daily.

Maybe we will read the signs, catch God's eye, and hear the message.

We matter. Because God loves us.

Ultimately, that's all that really matters. In spite of our missteps en route. In spite of the swirling words and voices around us.

We matter. Because God loves us.

TRAVELING MERCY

Dear one,
Do you read me?
Hear me?
See me?
Just this one message matters:
I love you.
That's it.
The reason behind the entire season
That is life in this world.
Let my love guide your steps,
Quicken your pulse,
And speak into your longing,
Wanting soul.
I love you.
And you matter.
Love,
God.

NOTE TO SELF

Wait with the message.

CREATED AND RESTORED

"You will be like God."

—Genesis 3:5

The rest of creation was made "according to its kind." But God dreamed up humanity and said, "Let us make them in our likeness." Then the serpent popped up in the midst of the perfection, all hiss and spit, to taunt the twosome: "You would be like God if you ate that, and that's what God doesn't want." If only Adam and Eve could have replayed what they knew to be true—that God *created* them in the likeness of God. *God* did that. Already.

The serpent dangled a key to a room that in some ways was already open. Adam and Eve were in God's likeness, not in form but in mental and spiritual capacity, created to be vice-regents of the world. God wanted us to "rule over the fish in the sea and the birds in the sky, and over every living creature that moves on the ground" (Gen. 1:28). What more could we possibly want?

The rest of the human journey, the rest of the pathway, God would come alongside, constantly inviting the people originally created in his image to return to that image. For the bulk of the Scriptures, the means was perfection: become holy in order to be like God.

An absolutely impossible commandment, except for one thing: holiness is a moment-by-moment status. The more consistently we live in repentance, not dragging our own refuse into our nest but living a life of confession and forgiveness, cleaning house regularly, we approach holiness. Our relationship with God intact.

But even so, those rules for holiness were meant to be temporary. God's long-term plan awaited the perfect time for fulfillment, a timeline inscrutable by human minds and humanity's limited eyesight. Becoming like God would be the modus operandi, for those who choose it, with the birth of the Messiah, the long-awaited seed of Eve's body. The impossible became possible one morning when a rock rolled away from the opening of a tomb and revealed a yawning cavern. Empty.

The resurrected Christ would provide us the way back into the likeness of God. The Scriptures promise us that finding our way means conforming us to the image of Christ, who is the exact representation of God (see Heb. 1:3)—that we would look like Jesus, thus like God, on the inside. That we would have the mind of Christ (see 1 Cor. 2:16). That we would act like God in this world—vice-regents! This still short-circuits my limited brainpower.

According to Jewish tradition, Adam and Eve were suffused with light before they disobeyed. They were bright with God's brilliance, so they never noticed the naked state. Fascinating possibility. If so, the light went out after that bite of fruit. But we fast-forward to Jesus, the "radiance of God's glory" (Heb. 1:3), to Paul who said, "Let light shine out of darkness" (2 Cor. 4:6) And then, we shine like stars in the sky (see Phil. 2:15).

Light restored. Glory restored. Image restored.

And the unrelenting, tireless, faithful effort of our God to reestablish the hope of Eden in us continues today. A mercy, a stunning gift, absolutely undeserved. It's a miracle. The serpent doesn't win. And we aren't going to miss out, after all. Neither will the world. Not if we really live restored. Shining. Better stock up on sunglasses.

TRAVELING MERCY
Dear one,
We created you
To look like us
And act like us
In this world.
It's not too late.
It's the perfect time.
The way is still moment-by-moment,
But it looks like
Christ in you,
The hope of glory,
The radiance of my glory,
And you,
Starlight in this world.

NOTE TO SELF
Radiance is moment-by-moment.

THE EVE EFFECT

When the woman saw that the fruit of the tree was good for food
and pleasing to the eye . . . she took some and ate it.

—GENESIS 3:6

The word *sacrifice* isn't mentioned in the account of Eve
and her forbidden fruit foray. Nevertheless, she sacrificed a
lot for that bite. I don't believe she understood what she was
going to give up, though—it was all so new, and the idea of loss
was as foreign, as unknown to her, as clothes to a fish. Living
in a world without loss messes with my mind. I don't know how
to process that possibility, but Eve had never experienced
loss, never encountered need or want. All her desires were
100 percent met in idyllic Eden. And death? "You shall surely
die," meant nothing to her. It sure sounded ominous, but then
again, who knew? (The serpent and God, that's who.)

Eve had no idea what disobedience would cost in terms of
relationship with God. With Adam. With her own soul. But
also with the world and her body and the future and that sweet
place with a welcome mat that read "Home." In her innocence,
she couldn't run a risk assessment.

Sometimes, of course, a sacrifice is unwitting even if sin is
deliberate; the sacrifice given up without counting the cost,

without realizing the tremendous toll a broken heart and broken relationships could exact from the change purse of the soul.

With most sin, we underestimate the impact of our actions on others, even on people we have never even met. And on ourselves. The Eve Effect—the Jane Effect—the Everyone Effect—ripples throughout the world. Ultimately, Eve's losses were cataclysmic, and their unfolding left soul wrinkles that remain in our own DNA to this day.

Sin is one of the least popular topics in church. Who wants to talk about something so, well, judgmental? Who are we to decide that someone else needs to hear a message about sin? Who are we to point fingers? A valid question indeed—I must be willing to address my own sin if I am going to invite others to examine theirs. It's that log and splinter tale all over again (see Matt. 7:4–5).

But isn't that the good news? That even though Adam (and Eve!) sinned, and through them and thanks to them, but also through our own fault lines of the soul, so have we—even so we in Christ have all been made alive (see Rom. 5:12–14). We, the people of God, are alive because Christ's work cancels our sin. "I am the way and the truth and the life," Jesus said (John 14:6). This doesn't mean the sin doesn't exist, but the power attached to it has been zapped. Of course, of course we all miss the mark. No bull's-eye here; I'm not even on the target much of the time.

But we will get closer to the target, and maybe even land on the target, once we begin to recognize and own our brokenness that results in sin. What if, then, the Everyone Effect is one of holiness, one of such Christlikeness that it becomes not just a ripple effect but such a sweeping tide of lovingkindness and joy that the world takes notice?

What if? Just imagine. It sounds like Eden, just a little bit.

TRAVELING MERCY
Dear one,
The Eve Effect and Adam Effect
Affect everyone.
But the Jesus Effect
Changes everything.
Absolutely everything.
Sin no longer rules,
And shame is no longer the marker.
Rather, the marker is
The great gift of relationship
Ruptured by sin,
Repaired by Christ,
Restored in you.
Right on target.

NOTE TO SELF
Ruptured but repairing.

JANUARY 7

THE GATE

When the woman saw that the fruit of the tree was
good for food and pleasing to the eye, and also desirable
for gaining wisdom, she took some and ate it.

—Genesis 3:6

In the 1970s, William Safire, former speechwriter for then-president Richard Milhous Nixon, coined the term *Watergate*. The scandal involving the Watergate Hotel and two politically driven robberies in 1972 led to an investigation of the Nixon administration and the resignation of the thirty-seventh president of United States of America. Since then, the suffix *-gate* attached to a noun suggests a broad scandal.

The -gate has been applied to a wide variety of scandals, with particular resentment reserved for countries other than the USA that try to borrow our term for their own use. It's enough to make your chest puff proud, getting to be the country that claims the origin of such an illustrious and much-coveted term. Particularly, this suffix is used in government and politics, although the entertainment industry has a few notorious versions.

Might I propose the first, the greatest, the most far-reaching scandal in the history of the universe? The original scandal is almost as old as dirt and reaches to the ends of the earth, impacting every single human being, born and yet to be born.

Fruitgate.

The serpent tempted Eve with a twisted truth. She capitulated and ate the only food item forbidden to the first couple on an extensive menu. Her husband, who for some reason apparently wasn't around to help his wife avoid temptation, decided she'd gotten in on a pretty good deal and he wanted a cut. I mean, a bite.

She ate. He ate. And we all ended up with a bite of the big one: death. Death would come. Adam didn't die, immediately, at least not in the way the serpent suggested. He lived physically for 930 years, but the light of God within the couple extinguished. There began the atrophy of spiritual death and the forever-after longing for a life that would never end.

The consequences of Fruitgate were satisfied, many years later, when a man wearing sandals appeared and said, "I am the gate; whoever enters through me will be saved. They will come in and go out, and find pasture" (John 10:9).

Jesusgate. And scandal would riddle his life, and eventually, the political machine would attempt to destroy his life, just like in Eden. But this time? This time, death died and life lived again.

Today, when we're tempted by the latest fruit guaranteed to make us wise, to give us life, to make us feel a little more godlike, oh, friend, let's skip Fruitgate entirely and head straight to Jesusgate. With him, we go in and out, and find green pasture. No more Fruitgate.

TRAVELING MERCY
Dear one,
I've always intended
For *forever*
To describe your life.
Don't let the scandal of Eden
Rule your life.
The death and the path that began
At Fruitgate
Ends at the Jesus gate.
Come in, little lamb,
And find green pasture.
The way is open.

NOTE TO SELF
Choose the right gate. Walk in.

FROM GRIEF TO GLORY

The morning stars sang together and all the angels shouted for joy.

—Job 38:7

The moment of Eve's defiance was the beginning of the end. But was it also the end of the beginning? Both of these statements feel true: the beginning of the end of life as Eve and Adam knew it, however briefly; and, the beginning of the end of the wondrous days of creation. The beginning of the end of innocence and hope. And the end of the beginning, the end of the fresh newness of an unsullied world. The end of the beginning of the unfettered spiritual life, that just-born and barely experienced ability to be one-on-one with God, to make eye contact and perhaps—imagine!—even physical contact with the one true God.

This moment deserves its own grieving ceremony, a funeral procession, maybe even the rich, poignant trumpet tones of "Taps," guaranteed to start grief pealing.

Consider God's great sadness right about now. The heartbreak of watching your precious creation, the greatest gift ever conceived and the pinnacle of your creation, destroyed with a single swallow. A his-and-hers picnic on the lip of disaster. Oh, the grief in heaven, the sharp intake of heavenly breath, the angels gasping and unable to exhale. The weeping, for surely, there was weeping at this finale.

But what if it is yet another beginning of a beginning? The moment God found the couple in the garden, cowering behind their bush and clutching their itchy crumbling fig leaves—that moment God enacted the plan he actually put in place from the beginning of the first beginning.

And the world, spoken into being, would spin forward for centuries until the One who spoke in the beginning, spoke once again and walked about—just like God in the beginning-beginning—only this time becoming flesh and blood and offering the only remaining possibility of restoration and reunion.

Then we hear the strains of that magnificent love song from 1747, "Love Divine, All Loves Excelling," and Charles Wesley's final verse:

> Finish, then, thy new creation;
> Pure and spotless let us be.
> Let us see thy great salvation
> perfectly restored in thee;
> Changed from glory into glory,
> Till in heaven we take our place,
> Till we cast our crowns before thee,
> Lost in wonder, love, and praise.

At last, the new creation finished—the old creation sullied, but now, a new beginning. At last, the unimaginable and impossible perfect restoration of our image. Or rather, God's image in us. And that line, "Changed from glory into glory"? It is drawn from the verse, "But we all, with unveiled face, beholding as in a mirror the glory of the Lord, are being transformed into the same image from glory to glory, just as from the Lord, the Spirit" (2 Cor. 3:18 NASB).

From the glory of that beginning, through the glory of the law, and now, the glory of a life changed by Jesus Christ and powered and illuminated by the Holy Spirit. The process continues daily, glory to glory. And then one day, we shall be like Jesus, because we will see him face-to-face.

We choose, beginning today, another beginning. We choose change. We choose glory.

TRAVELING MERCY
Dear one,
Your shift from faded glory
To new glory
Replaces the grief in heaven
With great joy.
We rejoice over you,
Over our glory
Being found more and more
In you,
Shining more brightly
In this tarnished world.

NOTE TO SELF
Choose restoration.

THE COVER-UP

Then the eyes of both of them opened, and they knew
they were naked; so they sewed fig leaves together
and made coverings for themselves.

—GENESIS 3:7 NET

With barely a breath in between, fresh-squeezed shame and fear appear when the couple eats the fruit from the forbidden tree. Now wide-eyed to their own vulnerability, they become the world's first animal-friendly, vegan tailors. "No animals were harmed in this garment factory," their advertising could read.

Not animals, maybe. But those fig leaves are sticky and scratchy, and unless the couple wears the leaves itchy-side out, they're in for a rash of trouble with their leaf wear. It's a step up from poison ivy leaves, but fig leaves aren't kind.

The great cover-up continues for all of us throughout time as we attempt to veil our own vulnerabilities, our own rough edges. We try to disguise our sin and our unhealthy thoughts and actions.

Further, we always use materials inadequate for covering. We don't have a time-lapse camera, but maybe Adam and Eve grabbed the leaves closest to the site of their downfall. The small spread of a fig leaf might offer a bit of strategically placed cover. Like them, we will use whatever suits us, whatever excuses are at the ready.

In fig-leaf fashion, Adam blamed his wife—talk about an immediate outworking of poor choices. But I get this. Too often my first reaction is to shift the focus and responsibility to another person. Or situation.

We hide evidence and look over our shoulder to see if we're seen. We cover up by plastering a good deed on top of a bad one, hoping for a cancelation effect. We'll convince ourselves that others are far worse than we are, that their misdeeds reek to high heaven and ours only exude a slight stench, nothing a little fig-leaf cologne won't mask.

We decide that all's fair in love and war and getting our own way and making our own way. We'll blame our parents for their poor parenting. We'll blame our teachers or other authority figures who acted with such precise and blatant imperfection in our lives. We'll blame doctors, lawyers, God. Adam blamed Eve and Eve blamed the serpent and we follow suit. Others aren't blameless. But how long can we blame them? When is it time to shift the game to growth?

It's all a cover-up. Fig Leaf Effect. All to keep us from having to face our own, easily exploited, exceptionally vulnerable, horribly embarrassing nakedness—the state of our own soul that just had a blowout.

Adam and Eve never apologized, did they? Repentance is good for shame. It reestablishes the relationship ruptured by sin. It wouldn't have restored Eden, but it sets us free from our fig-leaf flimsiness and dis-ease, and the fear of being recognized in our nakedness.

Through repentance we find our way from fig leaf to forgiveness. If we confess our sins, 1 John 1:9 assures us, God "is faithful and just and will forgive us our sins and purify us from all unrighteousness."

And the next time, perhaps we'll recognize our cover-up tendencies and save ourselves from the rash.

TRAVELING MERCY
Dear one,
From fig leaf
To forgiveness
Is the best way
To find your way.
There will always be a reason
To shift blame.
But I am faithful
And will forgive you
If you just come to me.
No more cover-up.
Confession combats shame.

NOTE TO SELF
Reestablish relationship with repentance.

PRE-FALL TO FREE FALL TO FOOT RACE

> Then the man and his wife heard the sound of the
> LORD God moving about in the orchard.
>
> —GENESIS 3:8 NET

What to make of God, walking about the garden in the cool of the day? Adam and Eve, after all, have just wrecked life in the land of perfect for everyone. God knows this, yet nonchalantly strolls about hoping to catch the breeze, as though life on planet Earth hasn't just been corrupted. (Also, to assume that the heat bothers God is interesting. God with legs, walking? God sweating?)

The Hebrew word translated "cool" is *ruah*: breath, wind. With this insight, the passage begins to make sense. This is the God who set the winds in motion at creation's birth. This is the God who shakes the desert (see Ps. 29). Perhaps, then, this God is not just meandering through a garden called Pleasure, enjoying the falling temperatures and a sweet breath of air.

No, this is the God of all the earth, whose primo creation just purchased a bite-one, get-one-free ticket to exile. The hard drive of creation entirely corrupted, and the software too.

Using the original Hebrew word, we might instead say that God blew into the garden or God arrived with special effects worthy of Hollywood. *Ruah* can even be interpreted, "the wind in the storm." A roaring.

No wonder the couple hid. Even if it is a little ironic, as though this powerful God, the one who created the entire world that surrounded them, who handcrafted the man and woman, wouldn't figure out where they were? But their new awareness of their own state sent them into hiding. Not only were they cognizant of their nakedness; they were, suddenly, mindful of their great vulnerability and also, perhaps, a wee bit alarmed at God's mighty power.

So God blew up a storm to find Adam and Eve and was very displeased. When the Lord God called, "Where are you?" the word translated "called" might be more like a summons, as in, "Show up, front and center, right now."

The man tries a verbal covering. "I heard you moving about the garden." (I guess so, if God blew in on a storm.) This could be rendered, "I heard your powerful voice," and we are back to a "storm theophany," God revealed in a storm. "And I was afraid," the first man finished, like he'd run out of breath (Gen. 3:10 NET).

This upsets my normal placid interpretation of this passage—in a good way. For God to appear in a windstorm of grief and disappointment and even anger makes sense. There's the apex of God's creation, given the best in the world to enjoy, and it's over in a single swallow. Grief surely swirls around God like a maelstrom.

Parents grieve a child's sin. Of course God grieves, and must redirect, helping these children—the first man and woman, and us—find their way. They will have to find it apart from the

Tree of Life, for to eat from that tree would mean living forever in a state of moral death.

Thus begins the marathon of exile.

But the breath of God appears repeatedly throughout the people's travels—blowing apart seas, shaking deserts, and breathing life into old dry bones. Then Jesus arrives on the scene and breathes the Holy Spirit's breath (see John 20:22) into his people. God gives us God-breathed Scripture (see 2 Tim. 3:16) until that great day when we are all reunited in a new heaven and a new earth.

Honestly. It's enough to take your breath away. Until then, breathe deeply. Because the *ruah* of God is the oxygen we need to keep running this race.

TRAVELING MERCY
Dear one,
When you breathe
It tells your body and your brain
That everything will be OK.
So breathe in my breath
Fill yourself with my Word,
My Holy Spirit,
My life.
I promise resuscitation
Every step of the way.

NOTE TO SELF
Breathe deep. Run with God.

HIDING PLACES

They hid from the LORD God among the trees of the garden.

—GENESIS 3:8

Adam and Eve's reaction after that succulent bite of sin was the same as about any guilty child, myself included: They were startled at the sound of God. They were going to be found out!

With their knowledge of evil, the hair trigger set itself inside them, ready to fire at any provocation. That provocation appeared in a breeze—or a windstorm, depending on the interpretation. God's powerful voice sounded across the garden. They fled into hiding.

Their running was about them, not God. God wasn't evil and had acted only in kindness and generosity. Perhaps awareness of their own capacity for evil sent them running. The word *naked* in chapter 3 carries the essence of being exposed, stripped, and laid bare.

Here hiding isn't about the thrill of being found, like children playing hide-and-seek. More like the fear of being found, and found out, for various reasons. Fear of judgment—we'll be found lacking, our sin exposed. The jig will be up then—others will know our imperfections. But they'll also confirm what we suspected: We aren't even acceptable. We're entirely subgrade.

Then another fear leers at us: We desperately fear abandonment. Because we aren't perfect or acceptable, people might abandon us. So we hide our imperfections; we hide behind our happy-face clown smile. No one must know how messed up we really are—including ourselves.

That works super well. Unless you actually want a real relationship, with real live people, who have the option of leaving but choose to stay.

Top off these fears with the fear of harm and exposure. No wonder Eve and her man hid. Knowing good and evil, they saw both within themselves as well. That's enough to send them cowering for cover.

These reactions fire from the devastating effects of shame. Immediately, the sense of exposure and vulnerability forced the man and woman to cover up and take cover. However flimsy that leaf was (very), or how invincible (not), how grievous that they were afraid of the very One who wanted to protect them.

But we react the same way. In our shame and fear, we hide from God. We turn our backs on him, because he couldn't love us, couldn't possibly forgive us.

Adam and Eve didn't know how the story would end. They only knew that they had bitten off more than they could chew. And while they hid from God, though they didn't know where *they* were, God knew.

Only generations later would we recognize that we could stop hiding. We say with David, "You, God, know my folly;

my guilt is not hidden from you" (Ps. 69:5). Though our sins
have hidden us from God's sight, God's arm is not too short
to save (see Isa. 59:1–3).

Remember the Genesis 3 word for naked, with its sense
of being stripped and laid bare? Hebrews 4:13 agrees:
"Everything is uncovered and laid bare before the eyes of
him to whom we must give account." But we don't stop there;
we can't. We, who hide out of this drastic fear of exposure,
hear this amazing good news: "Therefore, since we have a
great high priest who has ascended into heaven, Jesus the Son
of God, let us hold firmly to the faith we profess. . . . Let us
then approach God's throne of grace with confidence, so that
we may receive mercy and find grace to help us in our time
of need" (Heb. 4:14, 16).

We find our way to God's throne. Hold firmly. Approach
confidently. Receive mercy. Come out, come out, wherever
you are.

TRAVELING MERCY

Dear one,
I see you hiding,
And I am the finding God.
Hear the good news:
My Son sounded the "all clear"—
No need to hide.
Come out,
Come out,
Wherever you are.
Come to us,
The mercy and grace
You've been waiting for.
Cover your shame.
No more need to fear.
Hear it again:
All clear.

NOTE TO SELF

Hold firmly. Approach confidently. Receive mercy.

FROM TOIL TO TREASURE

"Cursed is the ground because of you; through painful toil
you will eat food from it all the days of your life."

—Genesis 3:17

Pain where before there was no pain. Eve's disobedience forever compromised women's childbearing and marital relationships, two painful ripples of sin. The ground was cursed, because Adam, man of dirt, chose obedience to the taskmaster of his own appetite rather than obedience to God. "Don't eat," but Adam ate. Adam's bite of the forbidden food created painful toil, compromising forever our relationship with work. More ripples of sin.

I come from farmer stock—both grandfathers tilled, planted, and harvested. And while I remember the smile deep in their eyes, the joy on their faces because they loved the soil, I also remember the sweat of their brows. They worked physically hard, tending the earth. They suffered through failed crops, bountiful years, and all points in between.

Painful toil and cursed soil. A far cry—heart cry, soul cry, heaven cry—from God's original work order in Genesis 2:15: "The Lord God took the man and put him in the garden of Eden to work it and take care of it." Cultivating the soil wasn't part of the original deal. Just tending the land, working it. Only after the forbidden consumption would the provision of food entail sweat, toil, and tears. The cursed ground would forever make providing food for the family difficult.

Working the ground would require a lot more work. What a blow for agriculture through the ages—sticks and stones break more than bones. They'll break your plow blades and your spirit.

Then there's the invention of weeds—I'm not so sure they were part of Eden, because they seem to spring up or become problematic after Adam disobeys.

The invasion of weeds spelled potential death of crops, and then many centuries later another industry sprang up: herbicides. Some research shows that these chemicals would help control the weeds but further poison—curse!—the ground. It's possible that those very chemicals would become part of the destruction of the nutrient value of the food as well as the health of the ground, its workers, and consumers.

This trajectory is losing altitude. More sin, evident in the very dirt underneath our fingernails both physically and morally. The dust bowl tells its own tale of poverty-stricken farmers and lost farms due to improper farming techniques geared for mass production without tending properly the land's needs and characteristics. A glance around many areas in North America and we find fertile land buried beneath often-vacant strip malls, with imported foods in our grocery aisle.

To combat the curse of dumb-downed food, friends with farmer instincts started aquaponics on their southern patio. For their evening shift after demanding day jobs, they tend the fish and the piping and water supply. Within weeks they harvested leafy vegetables from the giant tubs outside the kitchen. Another couple has hydroponic lettuce growing in their basement. Both couples are reducing the food mileage and increasing its nutrient density. They're finding, once again, the delights of a garden called Pleasure.

They choose to fight against the curse. We can, too. Whatever we can do to help the earth and help our food sources helps us all. And we can work with one eye focused on the final chapter in the story: from the cataclysmic fall and the outworkings of sin, we come to the Christ, to the triumphant one-day-soon reign of the One who will create a new heaven and a new earth. One day Christ will cancel the curse in full.

One day. Meanwhile, we tend, we toil, we till. We *steward*. And we learn to sing. One day we'll bring in the sheaves.

TRAVELING MERCY
Dear one,
Whether it's lettuce
Or words
Or people
Or piles of paper
Tend, toil, till
Until I return.
I'm coming soon.
I promise.
Keep bringing in the sheaves.
It's a taste of the garden called Pleasure.

NOTE TO SELF
Eye on the goal.

FROM FOOD FIGHT TO FOOD FINALE

"By the sweat of your brow you will eat food."
—Genesis 3:19 net

The trees God planted in Eden were pleasant to the sight and good for food (see Gen. 2:9). This juicy detail reveals that God cared about the aesthetics of the world and could've made everything ugly but functional. Instead, the food would be gorgeous, appealing to the people not yet created.

Funny—not—how food and drink present such a presence in the opening chapters of Genesis. Food would prove to be a fundamental stumbling block for people, beginning in Eden, clear through today. Adam and Eve, surrounded by delightful delicacies, deliciousness in all shapes and sizes, opt for the one item in creation not listed on the menu. "Ah," they said. "it *is* lovely, and it will make us wise."

Food would become more than an issue of wisdom. It would become a source of connection, of spiritual and emotional sustenance and of security for people, as well as a primary source of addiction throughout the ages.

Starting with that buy-one-get-one fall in Eden, people would have to work hard for food rather than reach up and pluck it in year-round ripeness from trees. "Through painful toil you will eat food from [the ground]. . . . By the sweat of your brow you will eat your food," God told Adam (Gen. 3:17, 19).

Then right outside the door of Eden, there on the stoop with the heat of the flaming sword at their backs, the scent of the first garden still pluming in their nostrils, Adam and Eve had two boys who grew up and brought God offerings of food. Cain's was less pleasing than Abel's, and in the struggle for dominance Cain killed Abel. Part of Cain's consequence for the first murder in history was, "When you work the ground, it will no longer yield its crops for you" (4:12). In other words, "Food is going to cost you, buddy."

Skip ahead and we encounter Lamech naming his son Noah, meaning "rest," because this boy was expected to provide everyone rest from the painful toil of their hands, "caused by the ground the LORD has cursed" (5:29).

The flood sure did give everyone an opportunity to rest, at least those who actually trusted God enough to board the boat. The floodwaters would destroy everything, leaving behind a barren landscape that needed time to restart.

In spite of the pleasing aroma of Noah's first offering on dry ground, Noah's substance battle would erupt with wine. We won't hear of him again after his boys find him in a drunken slumber and the blessings and curses are doled out.

Clear through the Scriptures, food tempts people to fear, turn from God, hoard, and complain. Plus, without adequate food and nutrition, our brains don't function and our bodies stop cooperating. All systems eventually stop.

Our bodies run on food—it is our fuel. It is one of our delights. And our number one love substitute.

Thankfully, God doesn't leave us in our gaunt hunger for deep love, masked by our superficial longing for pleasures and tasty treats. God came to us, yet again. After providing forty years of wilderness manna and after feeding the Israelites throughout the centuries and placing them in a land flowing with milk and honey, God came, and still comes, to us in Christ who says, "I am the bread of life."

When we find our way to Christ, we begin our journey toward wholeness. We will, at last, eat and be satisfied. In Eden, we ate and died. In Christ, we eat and live.

TRAVELING MERCY
Dear one,
Take and eat,
But come to me first.
This is why you bless the food—
That I would be the source of your love
And your joy.
I would be the one to lead you to contentment,
Not the food.
So take and eat
And bless.
And bring your heart's needs to me.
I will satisfy your hungry heart.

NOTE TO SELF
Why do I eat? What am I hoping for?

THE G-FACTOR

Sin entered the world through one man, and death through sin,
and in this way death came to all people, because all sinned.

—ROMANS 5:12

A recent trial against a police officer for a shooting left an upset trail of rioting and looting and, for some, the feeling of being ignored and victimized. The process of the trial, the arguments, the press conferences—all of this hid the real event from public view, because not one of us was at the scene of the struggle. All I knew was that I wanted people's safety on both sides of the issue. I didn't want life to be lost.

Once I served on a jury, a most unsettling experience. I, along with a handful of other people, would determine and declare the defendant either guilty or not guilty. This responsibility kept me awake at night and made me jittery and terrified throughout the trial's proceedings: the testimony, interrogation, closing arguments, and pleas. And all day long for a week, the division in the courtroom separated a brokenhearted family from the group accused of malpractice.

How could I declare someone guilty? Or not guilty? I wasn't there. The only person who could decide on that verdict was dead and long buried, and while none of us wanted the possibility of malpractice to be repeated, a guilty verdict would change nothing in terms of the deceased. He wasn't coming back. All the money in the world might help the bereft family's financial loss, but it wouldn't make up for the absence of the loved one.

In the end, we ruled against the defendant, after hours of deliberation, sequestering, and some awful take-out/carried-in food. But I still feel the weight of that decision, so many years later. We, earthly beings who weren't even there at the critical moment, the life-or-death intersection, declared someone guilty. This continues to grieve me.

Any attempt to see justice done this side of heaven should leave us all with fear and trembling. The declaration of guilt or innocence should humble us greatly. For my own sins, I carry enough guilt for the entire human race.

From the beginning of time, when the possibility of sin existed in a perfect world, the costs of sin were clear and the judge of sin only One: God in heaven. God knows our struggles and knows that we constantly camp out near the door of temptation. God knows that with the slightest movement of our heart's trigger finger we, too, can dissolve into sin.

I will try to watch my own declarations of another's guilt, for daily I make decisions about people. They are harsh, they are unforgiving, they are angry or appalling or cold or lazy or meddling, or in good Southern terminology, "ugly." (In the South, where I come from, to call someone "ugly" is a character statement rather than a statement about someone's physical appearance.) I render judgment right and left—no trial, no cross-examination, no deliberation. I ask no questions, simply stamp someone with Guilty.

The only honest verdict for our own personal trial over sinfulness is always, always, always guilty, because we all have fallen short of God's perfect standard. We all have missed the center ring of holiness. And we only reach that center with Christ, through his death and resurrection, carrying our sins to the cross for us.

And, should we end up in the jury trying to determine another's legal innocence or guilt, may we be aware of our own proclivity toward evil and render judgment only with great prayer.

TRAVELING MERCY
Dear one,
Guilty, guilty, guilty.
Hear the gavel?
But hear this, now:
I have made a way.
You can escape temptation
At any given moment
By turning to me,
By inviting my Son
To stand between you and sin.
He has done it once for all time
And the pardon is full and free.
Just make your way to me.
And then listen again.
No gavel.
Only grace and mercy.

NOTE TO SELF
Make a "way of escape" plan.

PLEASE EAT

And he took bread, gave thanks and broke it,
and gave it to them, saying, "This is my body given
for you; do this in remembrance of me."

—LUKE 22:19

One Sunday I happened to be in church—actually, I am usually in some form of church on Sundays, just not always my home church. And this day was no exception. I was eight hundred miles from home, but I am learning to feel at home in any church where I worship God and hear his Word proclaimed.

This particular Sunday, we celebrated Communion. This sacrament moves me deeply, and even more so when I am able to actually partake of the bread. A little problem called celiac disease bars me from Communion because of the gluten-containing wafer or loaf. My heart literally sped up with anticipation when I learned that all the crackers were handmade gluten free from a gluten-free home. Blessed, broken, and given to all of us.

The privilege of celebrating Communion washed over me. The life represented in the elements overwhelmed me—the life of Christ, the death and resurrection, and Christ's final instructions on that last Passover meal. "As often as you eat this, remember me" (see Luke 22:19).

"Take and eat," the pastor proclaimed. "Take and drink." An invitation, a beckoning. Eat. Drink. Not *for* salvation but to proclaim salvation, the life we've taken into ourselves and attempt to live out through ourselves. To eat and drink having cleared our consciences through confessing sin and receiving forgiveness.

Such a far cry from the message at the tail end of the Eden experience: God's command, "Don't eat." And the serpent's insistence, "Aw, go ahead, eat it." With eating came death. With eating came sin, the essence of separation.

But this Sunday, eating reminded us of life. Even the word, *Communion*: with unity, together. Communion, broken in Eden, now represented by the act of Communion, eating bread and drinking wine together with our co-inhabitants on this garden called Earth. As often as we eat, as often as we drink, we're to remember.

Until when? Until Christ returns and shares the bread and the wine with us.

If Communion represents community, with union, together, then our unity in this worship service and in this world represents the miracle of God, reaching us again in Christ, inviting us to eat. To drink. To live and not die.

And our offering to this world is the same offering we receive during Communion. We return to the world and offer life. We offer bread to the hungry and juice to the thirsty. And we offer unity, the surprising gift of people who get along together. Not without conflict, but with peaceful approaches to issues and attitudes that could divide us and by refusing to be divided over divisiveness.

Until Christ comes again in heavenly glory. Until Christ returns and we live together, forever, in eternity. Never again separated as we were in the early days of the world's birth. God walking among us, together with us.

We of all people can offer this gift to the world. Take and eat. Take and drink. Live and don't die.

Take. Eat. Share. Repeat.

TRAVELING MERCY
Dear one,
The "Do not eat"
In the beginning was for your own good.
But now the invitation is on the table.
Eat.
Drink.
Love.
Live.
Share.
You'll show my life
To all you meet.

NOTE TO SELF
Receive and share. How hard is that?

FRAMED

The heavens declare the glory of God;
The skies proclaim the work of his hands.

—PSALM 19:1

Unbroken snow twinkled and glittered under the sun's bright gaze. I inhaled, filling my soul with the beauty outside the window. A brilliant cardinal swooped over the landscape then rested on a branch of the bare apple tree. I stood, captivated. And replete. The heavens declared and the snow declared and the cardinal declared the glory of God.

Though the day flew by like a ride on a luge, I carried with me the white-covered scene and the flashing beacon of a bird. Repeatedly, that beauty welled up within me, reminding me of the God who created beauty. Even now, the picture outside our window returns as a mini Sabbath, a tiny, life-giving personal retreat.

Whatever day of the week, however long, observing creation is one way to deny ourselves and do no work, as God commanded the Israelites, years after creating evenings and mornings and the seventh day of rest. Maybe we can't yet leap into a whole day of rest, but perhaps we can take little breaks along the way, when we notice the world around us and let it transport us into God's presence. Initiate a habit of rest.

It seems irrelevant to finding our way, this idea of a resting place, especially one prescribed and commanded. Doctor's orders. But freedom is found in resting when we enter into the depth of the Word. Rest means repose, and repose means trusting the foundation on which we repose to be firm, able to bear our weight, to hold us up.

Isn't that our bottom line? It's hard to stop working, because we trust in our work to get us to the next day and see us through the month and cover our bills and fix what's wrong with our lives. We don't trust others to bear our weight. We hear Paul when he said, "The one who is unwilling to work shall not eat" (2 Thess. 3:10), and the truth seeps into us with all the calmness of acid in our gut. If we don't work, we don't eat, we lose our house, our kids falter.

Honestly, that sounds more like prison than freedom. Freedom would be to recognize, every time we eyeball the beauty around us, that we depend on God for our well-being. And if God instituted the idea of a rest, maybe it is in that rest that we find our freedom.

If your life is like riding an avalanche, today, even if only for a moment or two, frame the beauty outside or inside; fix it in the eye of memory. Take a picture of the glory of the faces of people you love or the face of the moon or the face of the cardinal on the tree. Take a snapshot in the camera of your mind and create a scrapbook of mini Sabbath breaks.

Every time you view that gallery, see if your blood pressure drops and your heart lifts and the eyes of your soul turn back to the God who created it all. And the rest is your history and your present and your hope for the future.

TRAVELING MERCY
Dear one,
The heavens declared and the snow declared
And the cardinal on the tree declared
The glory of God.
And I declare—
I do declare!—
That I created all this beauty
For you
Because I love you.
I hope you notice it today,
Because in the seeing
Will come the knowing
That I love you.
I really, really love you.
And today,
I hope you'll rest in my love
And my sustenance.
Take a picture.
Do you see me
There in that frame
Loving you?

NOTE TO SELF
Frame beauty; store for future Sabbaths.

A WEEDING LIFE

Cursed is the ground because of you. . . .
It will produce thorns and thistles for you.

—Genesis 3:17–18

The garden flows along the chain-link fence.[1] Purple coneflowers, late-blooming bearded iris, and soft giant phlox bob in the breeze, brilliant and luminous in the early morning sun. Smaller plants cluster around the ankles of the showy giants, balloon flowers and others I can't even name.

Our neighbor chats over the fence, congratulating us on the beauty. This is a far different conversation from two years ago, when she rounded the fence line where I yanked baby walnut trees from the lawn.

"Please, Jane. Can't you do something about this border? Really. I'll even help."

Oh. Six-foot-high weeds towered, a bank of chaos rising from the soil. Crawly, creepy, and splintery weeds spread over the dirt and invaded the grass. I gulped.

How horrible and embarrassing. I could protest about limited funds and time, my travel schedule, an unwieldy life. We had worked on the rest of the yard, but this bastion of bristles remained a last holdout. The stubborn weeds reappeared days after pulling, so I ignored them from all ten possible vantage points.

Then a spiritual-depth friend said, "I'm pulling up my perennials. Would you want any?" I gazed at the lush beds, their beauty filling my eyes. "Why pull them out?"

"I want to invest my energy in people." Her choice to dig out the flowers spoke for her priorities and her progressively debilitating disease.

So I returned with vintage Suburban and spade. Soon over fifty plants filled the SUV. With the summer heat bearing down, the flowers would live short lives in their plastic bags and cardboard boxes. I weeded in earnest. Thirty lawn bags, a million blisters, and gallons of sweat later, the twenty-five-foot length stretched bare of weeds.

Within hours, I arranged, planted, and watered. Though I chafed under her words, my neighbor's pointed remarks about the weeds had forced me into action.

Sometimes I wonder if our accept-all-behavior political correctness is all that correct. We so rarely confront sin in our own lives, let alone others'. I'm forced to weed my own soul-garden usually only when the towering display of my sin hurts others, who call me to digging. Listening to my teeth-gnashing about a situation, a friend said, "Jane, you've been moaning like this for years. What will be different this time?" I was struck mute. She needed to call me on my refusal to weed. No longer could I avoid eye contact with the ugliness. I needed to dig in and root out.

But ugliness returns if not replaced with beauty. My perennial flower friend was helping me yank out my ugly reactions and replace them with changed behavior. I started listening more to the reasons crouched behind my exhibits of sin. Because of deep wounds, I'd learned defensive patterns that might keep me safe on some level. But sin remains sin, however legitimate its original pain, and my garden taught me that the sooner I got rid of the weeds, the less they rooted, re-rooted, and spread. The sooner I confess sin in a relationship, the less damage sin does. Repentance, that on-your-knees posture of humility, is good for the soul.

I spent a lot of time on my knees that summer digging out weeds. The perennials leave less room for bramble and briar. Without my neighbor's words, the ugliness might still linger. But now I bask in the results of her words, grateful for her honesty.

Imagine the world if we helped one another root out weeds.

The flowers bow their heads on gracious stems, a benediction in the wind. A silent thank you to those friends.

TRAVELING MERCY

Dear one,
Dig in.
Root out.
We'll work together.
And you should bring a friend—
Bring your church—
And let's have a go
At those towering weeds.
Time to replace the uglies
With beautiful blooms.
I'll bring the water.
And the bandages.

NOTE TO SELF

Weed. Seed. Water.

NOTE

1. A version of this devotion was printed as: Jane Rubietta, "A Weeding Life," *indeed* Magazine, May/June 2013, 5–6.

TRANSFORMING WORK

So the LORD God banished him from the Garden of Eden to
work the ground from which he had been taken.

—GENESIS 3:23

Adam's smooth and untried hands erupted into blisters.
Painful toil makes it easy to forget that work itself is not the
curse. There is a more than complicated relationship between us
and work. It is confounding and conflicted. We love our work.
We loathe our work. We substitute living our work for living
our life. We use work to boost our own image and our own
self-esteem. Work becomes both a common denominator and
a means of comparison, and also our entrée into conversation.
"Hi, what's your name? What do you do?"

Work becomes a means of self-identification. A source of
pride, a door of temptation, a means of discouragement, and a
forever reminder of our fall. Work becomes *work*. Sweat of the
brow. Even if it's psychological sweat or emotionally taxing,
work can be painful. Office workers often report higher levels
of exhaustion than manual laborers.

Since Eden, we tend to base our worth on our work, to
worry about work, and to believe that work somehow makes
us separate from and less dependent on God. In work we

encounter both our limitations and our strengths. We discover and utilize our gifts and talents. With work we fall prey to the seduction of the serpent: "This will help you feel good about yourself. Take, eat. Work, work. Work is your salvation. There you will find your meaning, your hope. Your god."

We find ourselves working in order to feel valued and valuable. Nothing like a paycheck, a "well done," or just a little sweat to reinforce work as worth.

When God created Adam from dirt and then put him in charge of tending the field, it seemed fitting. When God then cursed the dirt because of the dirt man, rendering work painful and filled with thorns and thistles, Adam raked and shoveled, weeded and hoed. He dug his own grave.

From dust he came, to dust he would return. That would be his lot in life. Scratching out a living from the dirt reminded him of his fall from glory and his final resting place.

But not necessarily so. Work is not an end in itself. If paying our mortgage is the point of our work, well, rethink. Work becomes a means of faithfulness to God but not faithfulness to our god. Work is a medium for learning our gifts and honing our skills. And it is a way that we give back to God and this world. The Jews interpret God's blessing and command "Be fruitful and multiply" literally, as in, have lots of babies. But also, to be fruitful in their gifts and industry. It calls them to find joy in their work and return that work as a gift to God, at the end of every day and at the end of every week. At sundown they gratefully give their work into God's hands and rest.

This is the work-around to the toil and sweat of work—to find joy in God's provision of work and to give our work to God every single minute of every single day.

TRAVELING MERCY
Dear one,
Your worth comes from me
Not from your scratching around
In the dirt of the earth.
Yes, you came from dirt,
But you are created for glory.
So when you give me glory
In the work of your hands
And even in the sweat of your brow
I'll transform you
In the midst of your work
From work to worship.
You won't believe
How work flies
When you're having fun.

NOTE TO SELF
Worship and work. Works for me.

THE END OF ABANDONMENT

"[God] will never leave you nor forsake you.
Do not be afraid; do not be discouraged."

—DEUTERONOMY 31:8

Winter fosters feelings of goodwill and peace. Anticipation and joy. Merry Christmas, Happy New Year, joyous season of light, fa-la-la. For some. For others, though, it means abandonment. People feel alone and lonely during a season that presumably celebrates community and relationship.

Abandonment. The sense of being on our own with no one in charge who cares. No one to support or protect us. Our vulnerability increases during winter, though winter has no monopoly on abandonment.

Hasn't this loneliness been around since Fruitgate? Didn't Adam and Eve hear that metal lock clanging behind them and raise their eyebrows? Surely they turned toward one another, fear hollowing their eyes. "What on earth do we do now? How will we ever find our way, alone?" Fear follows hard on the heels of abandonment.

When Adam and Eve covered themselves, the institution of abandonment began. They saw nakedness—felt shame— covered themselves. We often handle abandonment the same way. Covering is a reaction to the feeling of being uncovered, unprotected, vulnerable, abandoned.

Like Adam and Eve's cover-up, those fig leaves of excuses, we cover our own abandonment issues in various fig-leaf ways. We work harder. We curry favor from others. We suck up to or turn up our noses at people in authority. We bury ourselves in weight or try to disappear through weight loss, or cover up our flaws with flashy or expensive stuff.

Maybe our covering looks like defensiveness. I don't want someone correcting me, because it feels like an uncovering of my defects, which in turn feels like judgment.

To abandon, forsake, desert. If we feel abandoned, forsaken, and deserted, then by whom? We take the exile to mean, "You're on your own, baby. But who would send us such a telegram? Is this *God's* word to us? Or a message we've received throughout the long and sometimes lonely and frightening days of our lives, on this journey toward somewhere?

Though chronic since Eden, the sense of abandonment also has a personal source. Relationships on earth exacerbate abandonment, so we don't have to look very far to reinforce what we already feel. Sometimes those feelings trickled or waterfalled down from parents or significant loved ones. Some of us feel deserted by the system or the church or society in general or a people group in particular. When our expectations of others, including God, are not met, we tend to feel abandoned.

Abandonment issues begin to be resolved when we tell ourselves the truth. God exiled the first couple, but never abandoned them. The journey from Eden is not the whole story. It is the end of Eden, yes, but not the end of God

accompanying us every step of our way, through parched
desert and green valley, through disappointment and darkness
and light and laughter.

God's word to the Israelites is God's word to us: "The
LORD himself goes before you and will be with you; he will
never leave you nor forsake you. Do not be afraid; do not be
discouraged" (Deut. 31:8).

Never? How, then, can we stop believing the abandonment
lie? As we find our way, we can also find ways to experience
God's presence in the midst of dark days. If in silence you
hear God's love, then close your mouth. If music takes you
into God's presence, then sing. If movement stills your fear
and helps you focus on God, go for a walk.

And keep holding on to the truth. God goes before you
and will be with you.

TRAVELING MERCY
Dear one,
Believe the truth
Not the lie.
I will never, never
Withdraw my support from you,
Nor my presence.
Where you go,
I go.
Just watch for me.
I walk with you
Every step of the way.

NOTE TO SELF
Abandon fear. Find God.

THE YEAR OF OUR LORD

So the LORD God banished him from the Garden of Eden
to work the ground from which he had been taken.

—GENESIS 3:23

Regrets and shame cloaked Adam and Eve as they bundled themselves together and made their way toward the exit.[1] Eve wrapped her arms about herself and stumbled through Eden's gate, past the angel of the Lord brandishing the flaming sword. Off they went, travelers on an extended hike, destination unknown. How much terror whipped them forward? Did the element of faith ever enter into their exit and sojourn?

Today we still look ahead to all the unknowns. Maybe those unknowns weigh heavily. The knowns weigh heavily, for that matter. We know the baggage we've carted into this year. Such a burden, carrying our bundles of worry like sandbags on our shoulders and setting off on a year-long hike.

In the old days, people referred to the year as "the two-thousandth year of our Lord," for example. In our politically correct society, perhaps because of fear of offending others, we no longer talk about this being the "year of our Lord." But as we look ahead at months full of unknowns, over thirty-one million seconds of challenges and blessings, maybe it's helpful to reinstitute that terminology.

Isn't every year the year of our Lord? If that's the case—and it must be, because the Scriptures tell us that God is the same yesterday, today, and tomorrow—then isn't *this* God's year, just like last year was? Is God somehow less God than last year? Does this year somehow belong less to God than last year did? We have a longer track record of God's faithfulness than Adam and Eve when they fled Eden.

So, if this is the year of our Lord, then don't all those unknowns belong to the God who knows? The future isn't hidden from God, though it is certainly hidden from our view. We know the problems at hand, but we haven't the faintest idea how or when or even if those problems will be resolved. And thankfully we don't have any sense of the troubles lurking beyond the next craggy outpost.

We can heave those sandbags full of unknowns onto God's shoulders.

And if this really is the year of our Lord, then we don't have to worry about all those millions of seconds ahead of us. That's really borrowing tomorrow's troubles for today anyway, as though we can do anything about them in advance. The only second we have to worry about is this one. Surely, if the year is God's, then this single second of time is also God's. We can say yes to that.

TRAVELING MERCY

Dear one,
You may have left everything you know,
But I know you,
And you know me,
And I know the plans I have for you.
I will show you.
I will bring you to the land.
I will provide for you
In this year of your Lord.
This year is mine,
And you are mine.
And for now
Perhaps that's all you need to know.

NOTE TO SELF

This second and tomorrow are God's problems.

NOTE

1. Portions of this devotion appeared as: Jane Rubietta, "The Year of Our Lord," *indeed* Magazine, March/April 2014, 2–3.

IN EXILE

So the LORD God banished him from the Garden of Eden.

—GENESIS 3:23

Exiles. A worldwide people group called human beings, so carefully created in Eden and so long gone from that would-be home. No matter who we are, no matter where we live, no matter the job we hold, no matter the size of our mortgage or rent payment, we all live in some form of exile. We don't recognize the gaunt, homeless look on others' faces or even in our own reflection, but the soul doesn't lie.

The lifesaving exit from Eden set in motion a lifelong exile for all of humanity. Adam and Eve exiled. Cain exiled from his family, condemned to wander. And on through the ages, we would be a people ever seeking home and never quite finding it in this world. A community of transients, people taking surrogates and substitutes for home, trying to find our home in others, in buildings, in material goods, in our work. And none of these, forevermore, would satisfy this deeply seeded and seated longing for a permanent home.

We would be nomads, with sand in our shoes and worn of soul, exhausted from the journey, from the time of Adam and

Eve clear through today. Tracing our unsettled journeys through Abraham and Sarah, their son Isaac, his sons, and their sons, through generations of offspring.

And then, in the middle of this eternity of exile, would be born One who left his home in heaven and came to earth in the usual way of pain and blood. As a baby he was carried off into exile by his parents to escape Herod's murderous plans. The Scriptures tell us that Jesus "tabernacled" among us—Jesus, who knew the glories of heaven, exiled himself. The Greek word means "to make one's dwelling," to live, to dwell, to spread a tent. John 1:14 reads, "The Word [Christ] became flesh [human, incarnate] and made his dwelling [tabernacled] among us." Jesus tabernacled, tent-camped, like one of the millions of refugees in this world.

But no angel barred the gate for Jesus. His was a willing departure from heaven's glories to earth's tenement housing, this ramshackle existence built like a child's Bible school craft of rickety hopes and planned obsolescent materials. He took on our flimsy shelter of flesh and blood, of feeble bone and sinew, and lived with us, lived like us, lived *for* us. Heaven's glory in earth's mud-made humanity.

Christ's exile from heaven would end our own homelessness forever. He would promise his disciples, and now promises us, that he returned to heaven to prepare a spot for us: "I go and prepare a place for you . . . that where I am, there you may be also" (John 14:2–3 NKJV)—a dwelling, a home, a welcome mat and keys for the door in glory. No more exile, not ever, once we leave earth's shore and shove across the river to the distant banks of heaven.

The exile from Eden would be completed by the exile from heaven, an exile that would open the way for us to reenter. For you, for me, for our neighbors in tents and in cardboard shacks and in the mansion down the street. Maybe we could look ourselves and others in the eye and simply ask, "Are you looking for home?" And then offer a map and a hand to hold.

TRAVELING MERCY
Dear one,
Take my hand.
Let me lead you
To my Son,
To our home,
To the hope of today
And of tomorrow.
You are no longer in exile
When you make your home
In us.

NOTE TO SELF
Find home. Invite others.

TAMING THE GREAT AFRAID

No temptation has overtaken you except what is common to
mankind. And God is faithful; he will not let you be tempted
beyond what you can bear. But when you are tempted,
he will also provide a way out so that you can endure it.

—1 CORINTHIANS 10:13

Fear of death, public speaking, ladders, black cats. Fear of
flying, the dark, lightning, spiders. And snakes. Snakes are
often mentioned in the Great Afraid Listings and topped out
the livescience.com list as the number one phobia.

Ophidiophobia, fear of snakes. A widespread symbol of
dislike and even disgust, with some terror sprinkled in for added
flavor. Snakes represent the stuff of nightmare and legend.
Mesmerized by the snake's fiery red eyes and soothing lure,
Mowgli in *The Jungle Book* ended up wrapped in the boa's
muscle-bound coils. Indiana Jones portrayed a courageous man
with one significant failing: fear of snakes. However much
myth surrounds this species, never underestimate the power
of a snake.

Even though some religions revere the snake as a symbol
of fertility or rebirth, most people don't want to dream about
them.

Psychologists trace the fear of snakes back to the life or
death instincts during early human history, when the ability

to spot and distance oneself from a snake meant the continu-
ation of your family line (not to mention your own life).
But I would trace it even further back. Snakes have tormented
us, inducing fear since Eden, right after Adam and Eve capitulated to the serpent's temptation. We've been alternately
succumbing and running ever since, though the face of temptation changes.

And isn't there an ancient reason for this? When the serpent
tempted Adam and Eve, its curse would be to crawl on its belly
all the rest of its days. Forever after, people would fear snakes.
Their low profile and smooth, quiet speed make them stealthy.
They strike before we're even aware of their presence.

While the idea of being hypnotized by a snake is a myth,
I fear we've been mesmerized by the idea of snakes as pets.
Not literally—although people try to own, cage, and tame
snakes—but rather, by the seductive power of its representa-
tive. Because of its smooth delivery of temptation to Adam
and Eve, the snake typifies the lure of temptation. It is suave,
seductive, and powerful. Temptation whispers in a soothing,
convincing voice, "This one won't hurt you. If God really is
good, then he would never want you to miss this wonderful
opportunity. Something that feels this good—or looks or
sounds this appealing—can't be bad."

Snakes seduce us. We imagine that we can tame a snake,
bring it home, cage it, and it will remain content and we will
remain safe. But there is nothing safe about a snake. To imagine otherwise is like playing with knives. We could just as
soon make fire our friend, but you cannot tame fire and you
cannot tame snakes.

But the age-old principle for survival with literal snakes works for us with the figurative snakes of temptation: identify the snake, have a plan for avoidance or escape, and know what to do for a snakebite. With God's power, we can learn to name the temptations belly-crawling toward us. With the help of the Holy Spirit, we resist the Devil. He will flee from us. God promised.

TRAVELING MERCY
Dear one,
Finding your way
Includes going through
And around
Temptation.
Keep your guard up
Against the Evil One
Because temptation
Disguises itself
As your favorite
Indulgence
And your greatest
Love.

NOTE TO SELF
Name, plan, and pray past temptation.

JANUARY 23

ROAD ROUTING

This is what the LORD says—he who made a way through
the sea, a path through the mighty waters . . .
"Forget the former things; do not dwell on the past."

—ISAIAH 43:16, 18

We've been trying to find our way since Adam and Eve
and their exodus from lush Eden. Immediately, they hit every
major transition on the stress scale. They lost their future, home,
perfection, health, and life expectancy. Their relationship
changed to one of blame and their self-perception to one of
shame.

With that angel outside Eden, to turn back would have
meant death for them, and so they forged forward, with a new
job description and the curse of being travelers rather than
garden dwellers. Theirs was the ultimate transition. They left
everything behind and started over.

They lost a literal paradise because of their sin. We leave
what often appears to be paradise for any number of reasons.
But it's loss just the same.

Maybe that's you. You've left everything. Yours is a saga of
loss, of relinquishment, perhaps willing, perhaps not. But letting
go of the past and the trappings of the past, which may have
looked like an Eden, is part of finding your way. *Trappings*

is an apt word, because our past and all that we had gathered
and accomplished, all our successes and achievements, all
our trophies and glowing rewards, perhaps even all our plans,
can easily become traps for us. All too often we aim for our
own vision of success, happiness, a rewarding life, not God's,
and that vision becomes our snare. Sometimes, it takes a
desert to set us free.

It's not an easy journey. Certainly not one people covet,
at least, not with foresight. With hindsight, perhaps, but that
is something saved for when many grains of sand have
slipped through the hourglass and the accumulated wisdom,
gleaned from desert travel, adds a richness to our souls.

For now, we know we are not alone. We leave yesterday
and last year behind, and like Adam and Eve, we start out
for a destination yet unknown. The footprints before us are
few, and the blowing winds of life quickly erase them. Still,
we have a testimony. By God's grace alone, the travel did
not undo Adam and Eve, nor did it destroy their descendants,
the Israelites. The journey, rather than becoming their undo-
ing, became their doing. Their sojourn began to make them
into the people they were created to be.

Today, so fresh to the wilderness, tender of foot and soul,
we know this: Though God didn't let Adam and Eve return
to Eden, he still had a plan. Even with Adam naming his wife,
we find hope and purpose. Though she would eat and we
would all die, after the fall and curse Adam named her
"mother of all the living."

God has a plan for us as well, and for today we choose to
stay the course. We can't go backward to last year or to the

past decade or to some wishful-thinking time behind us. Going backward is an option only in fairy tales and time-traveling mythology. We can only go forward.

If you find yourself trapped between yesterday and tomorrow—who doesn't; change is universal and ongoing—may you find yourself squarely in the hands of the Faithful One. Whether in heat or cold, in sun or dark, with our lurking fears and sneaking uncertainties, we hold this to be true: "The one who calls [us] is faithful, and he will do it" (1 Thess. 5:24).

TRAVELING MERCY
Dear one,
You can trace my hand in your life,
My plans for your life,
Up to this very day.
But do not look backward
Expecting to repeat or return
To the past.
For that is a snare to you.
Look forward,
Look into my eyes,
And follow my lead.
The way is wild,
But I am still the God
Of the wilds,
The One who makes a way in the desert
And streams
In the wasteland.

NOTE TO SELF
Find freedom in God's faithfulness.

DOORBELL

But in your great mercy you did not put an end to them or abandon them, for you are a gracious and merciful God.

—NEHEMIAH 9:31

Doorbells echoed through the almost-empty apartments and tiny houses. My friends had never delivered food baskets before, let alone to people in such dire straits, but they knew the season spelled despair for many in the disadvantaged neighborhood. Whatever the path to that threshold, the people on the list were one step away from eviction.

Eviction feels like an ugly word. It even sounds mean, the "ev" at the front hinting at the word *evil*. A hard, leering, menacing sound, like a demon hissing. Or a serpent.

Eviction conjures up scary scenarios of vindictive landlords with shaking fists hurling tenant belongings onto the lawn. Destroyed apartments and houses, unpaid rent and mortgages. Signs on doors, a big red X. Police officers escorting people away. On either side of the order, eviction spells trouble and troubled.

Eviction is a word filled with despair, with life gone wrong. The black-and-white images of families in the Great Depression, who lost everything in the stock market crash and the economic disaster, haunt us with the enormous loss involved. Of self-worth, of dignity, of hope.

Life gone wrong. Sounds about right, when we consider Eden. Despair and shame. Rock-bottom credit rating and the impossibility of rebuilding or renting or buying, of getting a fresh start. Nonpayment destroys people's trust. And eviction's emotional, personal equivalent: being unwanted, thrown out, a complete failure.

But eviction isn't the final answer; eviction is the catalyst for God's presence in a new and complete way.

In the closing of the garden of Eden, eviction and mercy seem to be mismatched traveling companions. Oxymoronic even, at cross-purposes with one another. Eviction being bad, mercy good. But here, mercy and eviction are surprising complements.

The word *mercy* is rooted in a Latin term meaning "price paid" or "wages." Webster's defines *mercy* as "a compassion or forbearance shown especially to an offender or to one subject to one's power." We see mercy lived out through God's eviction of the first couple, because they would be removed from the possibility of living forever in a death-state of sin. Compassion, forbearance to an offender or subject.

With the tenant eviction from the garden, God offered mercy. A holy hush covers this.

That winter's day when handing out the food baskets, my friends were unprepared for the empty eyes that first greeted them, for the embodiment of the desolation they'd only read about in the news. Nor were they prepared for the hospitality immediately offered. In the presence of mercy, doors swung open, faces lit up, and eyes brightened. Mothers wept. Fathers beamed. Children danced. Hope returned, if only for those moments, as the recipients embraced the gifts before them.

And this is, indeed, mercy. We are all like the families on the mercy basket list. Mercy for us all: hope given, penalty withheld. God is the knock at the door, the mercy basket brimming with kindness. And we are the people, beaming, dancing, and hoping once again.

Eviction, yes. Our address changed, but God's compassion remains unchanging. Throughout the rest of the Bible and to this very moment, God draws people back to compassion and urges them forward to the hope and the reality of restoration. Ours and the world's.

Mercy baskets, right to their door.

TRAVELING MERCY
Dear one,
Eviction? Yes.
Penalty? Yes. No.
Life forever.
Your repentance leading to restoration.
Compassion renewed,
Hope at the door.
Find your way,
Answer the bell.
You will find me
Waiting for you
Mercy brimming.

NOTE TO SELF
Mercy waits. Open the door. Share with others.

THE NEXT BEGINNING

"With the help of the LORD I have brought forth a man."

—GENESIS 4:1

After giving birth three times without painkillers, I wince thinking about Eve's delivery. Calling him Cain, which means "brought forth, acquired," she sounded almost surprised, like, "Whoa, wait, what just happened? What have we got *here*?

"Look! A small version of us, honey. Imagine that! Except, he has your parts, not mine. And also, why is he all scrunched up and red? What's with that cord-thingie hanging out of his belly? We don't have that indentation in us."

Then, after the agony died down a bit: "What was with all the blood? I haven't seen anything like that except when God slaughtered the animals for our clothes." She looked like she'd swallowed a rake, pained by the memory. Then, a few breaths later, after she rested and thought back on the birth experience: "And also, so sorry I nearly wrenched off your fingers—I don't know what all that pain was, but let's avoid repeating that."

Insight dawned. She dragged more air into her lungs. "Was *this* what the Lord God meant by those menacing words, 'I will make your pains in childbearing very severe; with painful labor you will give birth to children'?" (Gen. 3:16). Her mouth turned downward, an upside-down smile, the wonder mingling with the vapor of loss, of what might have been. "I think that qualified."

Then when her milk came in, her breasts sore and lumpy and the size of cantaloupes, she swatted at her mate: "Don't touch me! Get away! Ouch! Do *not* let that baby near my breasts, Adam. Do something." Where's the nursing specialist to tell her about latching on and sore nipples and breast infections?

No sitz baths, no doughnut blow-up pillows, no one to coax and coach her through kegels and post-delivery uterine contractions. No mother to stand over her, saying, "You'll be OK. One of these days your hormones will stabilize. One day your stamina will sneak back. One day Cain will sleep through the night. We all have gone through this. You'll make it, too." No one who really got it, the thrill and depth of love for an infant and the awful bleak exhaustion of too much baby and too little mama.

It strikes me as horrifically lonely, all the unknowns, so much loss of community already. No one to talk her through morning sickness, inferno-flashes, or hormone ignition.

The first woman. The first conception. The first pregnancy. The first time, ever.

And the fading of the glory of what was. Surely on the threshold of pregnancy and childbirth she remembered where they'd been, but did it turn into a sepia-toned nostalgia, she and Adam peering over the past like it was ancient family history? Or was the grief still as fresh as yesterday's lilacs, pain layering over pain?

And what was it like for the angels, for God in heaven, to watch this whole process? Delight mixed with grief? Because God should've been present for this miracle, in person, just like before, back in the garden.

But now, everything had shifted. And God looked ahead, heaven-rending and heaven-sending hope, for now the process began. The Messiah would come, seed of this woman and this man, the first ever. The next beginning had begun. And the best was yet to come.

TRAVELING MERCY
Dear one,
You feel alone
In the midst of such unknowns,
And your grief is great,
Your loss tangible.
But heaven is coming
Back to earth
One day soon.
So hold on to me,
Even unseen,
And each other.
Truly the best
Is yet to be.

NOTE TO SELF
Not alone. Not without hope. Holding on.

THE WORK REWARD

So I saw that there is nothing better for a person than
to enjoy their work, because that is their lot. For who can
bring them to see what will happen after them?

—ECCLESIASTES 3:22

When our kids were old enough to have distractions and temptations which we preferred they avoid, we encouraged (and charged) them to find some gainful, income-producing work in the neighborhood. People needed lawn care, mothers' helpers, dog walkers, and house sitters. We didn't want spoiled, gimme-that children. We also wanted the children to learn the value of good, honest, and hard work. We hoped they would build relationships with positive adults and develop a strong work ethic. We figured that just maybe they would discover some interests for their future (or some things they didn't want to do).

Depending on the child in question, this mandate was met with both groans ("Stupid Lawn Work Folder," screamed a manila file label during one child's tween years) and with industry. Later, that same child's journal read, "Yeah! I get to earn some money today!" Cash-in-hand ended up as a sweet incentive, but eventually the satisfaction of good work well done became a reward. Well, sometimes.

Occasionally we worked to convince them that work wasn't a curse, especially once we were voted the worst parents in the universe. Few of their friends were expected to work. Some didn't even do chores at home.

Since Adam, people would loathe their work or find their entire identity there, believing that without meaningful work, life was meaningless. But beyond that, *they* were meaningless. "Work makes the man" or woman, perhaps, which is tragic when work or the economy disintegrates, or in instances of underemployment or unemployment. Too, there's an element of work as atonement: This is the fallout. I owe this work because I sinned in Eden. *Sigh*.

Still others would overwork in order to prove themselves to others, or just to themselves. One friend took to sleeping in his office, working such long hours that driving home seemed senseless. In order to disguise his work habits, he brought a change of clothes to work and switched before the other employees arrived. His boss could never understand why he had to hire two people when our friend left that job.

Work, a snare. Love it or hate it, we would be stuck with sometimes-painful toil.

But work also became a means of identity, though not in terms of finding one's entire value and self from work. But rather, discovering identity by finding joy in work, work that uncovers your gifts and talents. A friend who oversees an assembly line never expected years ago that her necessary foray into the work force would push her to become a stronger woman and a mighty leader. People come to her for direction. Managers put her in charge, and she says with joy,

"I love my job." She discovered herself there: that she is gifted, strong, and can contribute in good ways to others' lives, the industry, and society.

Ultimately, she learned a secret emphasized by Paul long ago: "Whatever you do, work at it with all your heart, as working for the Lord, not for human masters, since you know that you will receive an inheritance from the Lord as a reward. It is the Lord Christ you are serving" (Col. 3:23–24).

That secret might have helped Adam, so fresh from Eden and the warmth of God's presence. But it's not too late for you and me.

TRAVELING MERCY
Dear one,
To see you
Work with your heart
Directed toward me,
Even if the work is not joyful,
Gives me joy
And changes your heart too.
You're serving me
And serving me with joy,
And I sure am joyed
With you.
May my joy
Be your strength
This day and everyday,
In and out of work
And life.

NOTE TO SELF
Will work for joy.

A LIVING FROM OUR LIFE

Cain worked the soil.

—GENESIS 4:2

Buckthorn trees clustered against the fence line, sending bunching roots up and down the hill in our yard. In our crazy busyness, we'd neglected those saplings. The saplings, of course, thrived, sending out more roots and shooting new trees into existence. Their roots thickened and their stems turned from wispy sticks to sturdy, thick trunks. They clustered together in little gossipy crowds of thorny trees. Subversive at heart, they backed into corners, particularly hard to attack with saw or ax. By the time we realized the trees' tenacity, a forest of them hedged our fence line. Talk about industry.

For a year, my husband toiled at those nasty buckthorns with a handsaw, eventually wielding pickax and shovel to attack and dislodge the roots. Invited into the aerobic exercise, I developed a decent swing of that double-pointed pickax. We worked through one-hundred-degree heat and fifteen-degree cold, red-faced and aerobicized from exertion.

Then we realized that walnut trees functioned in similar hostile-takeover fashion, and for the next year we hacked and sawed and axed and dug out those trees. By then the buck-thorn tried to stage a comeback for dominance, and the cycle rebooted.

This was entirely our fault—cursed was the ground because of us. And the fallout of that fault occupied and pre-occupied us for years. We sustained more than a few muscle injuries and aching backs, pulled tendons and strained necks.

Sadly, leading up to this, we'd been working so frantically trying to stay afloat in our primary calling—its own painful effort!—that we hadn't noticed the marauding trees. There was no tending and working the ground possible, not in our ministry and not in our yard.

Part of the curse is that work would be toil. Even if we love our work, wresting a livelihood from our labor challenges us all. College graduates wonder if they'll get a job at all, let alone in their dream calling, and if they'll ever chip away at their debt. One pastor, called to ministry as a second career, left a lucrative upwardly mobile position and enrolled in seminary. Now a few years into the pastorate, his student loans are so high and his income so low he's taken a second job.

So as we try to harvest meaning from the soil and from the work of our hands, one daily challenge will be to remember and to focus. We struggle, sometimes, to remember that work was not the curse and to remember why we work in the first place. Work is not just a necessary evil. Nor do we work simply in order to eat (since, unless you inherited a fortune, life requires income), but because work provides us with meaningful activity. It keeps body and brain in training. It invites interaction with others.

And significantly, work allows us to contribute to the well-being of the world. It is all part of being fruitful and multiplying, God's original command.

Ultimately, the curse will not win. We just have to remember that, when those buckthorn trees appear. We can thrive in spite of the curse. And in the fight against the thorns, we will keep our fighting shape. It's all part of finding our way through pain.

TRAVELING MERCY
Dear one,
The thorn trees will take over
Your life and your yard
If you let them.
But the thorns don't win.
I know how the story ends,
And so choose with me
To develop your swing,
To work the field
And plow the land.
Invest in the fields before you,
And you will grow.
You will wrest a living
From this life.

NOTE TO SELF
Work becomes both a living and a giving.

THE ONLY OFFERING

In the course of time Cain brought some of the
fruits of the soil as an offering to the LORD.

—GENESIS 4:3

The first child's birth brought joy and mystery, and
undoubtedly confusion. How do you raise a child? You've
never even seen a child before, and were never one yourself.
Adam and Eve were entirely without any frame of reference
for this new role.

A little brother soon toddled after Cain.

His name is our first hint that all is not well outside Eden.
With Abel's naming, foreshadowing lends a dark tone to
events that surely had the angels singing and marveling.
(They've never seen the tireless and timeless miracle called
birth, either. This is all new to both heaven and earth.) Abel
is a tenuous name, a wisp of a name, meaning "vapor," like
a morning mist that soon blows away.

Even without parents or parenting books, Adam and Eve
raised their boys. Their two sons managed to grow up and
find their own fields of work. In direct contact with the results
of the curse, Cain cultivated the ground, hacking into the
runner roots of thorns and thistles, the raw pricking reality of

a disadvantaged earth. Little brother Abel tended the flocks.
Flocks and fields. Life on the farm progressed.

So did their consciences, and their conscious awareness
of God. In the next breath, the brothers brought an offering
to the God of their parents, the God of creation, the God
responsible for everything as far as their eyes could see.

With those first offerings, Cain and Abel indicated a longing for God, and a desire to be in relationship. They must
have felt God's closeness, though not like their parents did
in Eden, and they wanted to please this God. While a sacrifice
implies a placation—pleasing God suggests there's a reason
God might not be pleased, and maybe these offerings would
help—their desire for community with God was a good sign.
Their offerings acknowledged God's presence and authority
in their world.

With this one act of bringing offerings, the truth presents
itself into our world of political correctness and deference to
others' belief sets: People want God. It was true right outside
Eden, with no organized religions and no lists of doctrinal
beliefs. People want God; people will seek God.

Throughout history, we would be a people trying to find
God. Whether through work or overwork. Through serial
relationships. Through creativity or building projects (Babel,
anyone?). Through acquisition of power. Maybe through
prayer and supplication, acts of penance, or self-denial.
Through achievement or withdrawal from achievement.
Behavior has meaning, and the meaning behind so much of
our behavior displays longing. Longing for connection, longing
for sufficiency. For relationship, for wisdom. For God.

Offerings, through work or play, through function or dysfunction, talk about our soul state. Whether deliberate or unconscious, our offerings speak: we want to prove ourselves adequate. We want Eden. We want God.

And we want God to accept and love us. Our hearts are broken and show themselves in our broken offerings and broken motives for offerings. Maybe God will love us if we make an offering.

We're far afield from the truth. Because God's love is bigger than our burnt offerings. God sees through our feeble gifts and motives for them. And loves us anyway.

TRAVELING MERCY

Dear one,
As you try to find your way
Back to me,
I am already loving you.
So head in my direction,
But it won't secure my love.
My love for you
Is far bigger
Than your inadequacies.
You've had my love
Since the first day of forever.
Just bring yourself.
That's the only offering
I could ever want.

NOTE TO SELF

What do my offerings say?

THE BEST GIFT

On Cain and his offering [God] did not look with favor.

—GENESIS 4:5

Cain worked in the fields, and Abel worked with the flock. Together they learned to hoe their own rows outside Eden. The first sons, first brothers, first farmers. And the first recorded people to present an offering to the God of their creation.

From Adam and Eve, they'd learned the story of falling short, of God's judgment on the land. Maybe they figured they'd better appease this God of the earth, because God sure cast out their parents. So after a time, they brought God offerings. Sensibly, the brothers' offerings reflected the work of their hands: Abel brought an animal offering and Cain a grain gift. What else would they have to give God, after all?

This makes sense. They didn't know any rules for offerings at this point and had no precedent in case law to witness to the right or wrong way to offer, or the right or wrong type of offering. They brought what they could. How can you bring what you don't have?

The good girl in me happily embraces God's response to Abel and his offering: God looked with favor. Whew, what a relief.

But relief is short-lived. Dread rolls over me at God's reaction to Cain and his offering. Not pleased. Not pleased. Not pleased. An endless chorus of displeasure circling around my brain. I feel an inward grinding of teeth and wringing of hands. Not pleased. Cain brought what he could and it wasn't good enough. This strikes too close to home, too much like our own reality: never quite good enough, always slightly inadequate.

But God's displeasure wasn't about the type of offering. Leviticus 2 instituted the grain offering. Cain's gift of grain was suitable in itself. His gift of heart, however, somehow displeased God. "On Cain and his offering God did not look with favor" (Gen. 4:5).

The heart of their offerings indicated their own soul state. It's been true since Eden. God didn't want or need the offering. But we need to offer, because in doing so, we acknowledge our humble position. An offering represents an internal bowing to God, manifested by the gift we bring. But the gift is not the bowing, and God's displeasure over Cain's gift teaches us about our own heart. It seems Cain's offering came from wrong motives.

An offering offers a genuine acknowledgment of how messed up we really are, how deserving God is, and how undeserving we are. God doesn't want our sacrifices. God wants our whole heart. David really got God's heart, many years later, as David repented of grievous sins, including adultery and murder. "You do not delight in sacrifice, or I would bring it; you do not take pleasure in burnt offerings. My sacrifice, O God, is a broken spirit; a broken and contrite heart you, God, will not despise" (Ps. 51:16–17).

I'm afraid I'm much more like Cain, often coming to God in hopes of proving to be good enough, than David, who came to God bent with humility and grief over his sinful state. I want to put in my time, to slap a little payment onto my overdue accounts. Whether it's a few bucks in the offering plate or volunteering for a group of disadvantaged people, it's easier than opening the ledger of my soul and issuing a warning: "Danger. Radioactive waste inside. But it's all yours. Clean me up, God."

It's too late for Cain and Abel. But there's still time for us.

TRAVELING MERCY
Dear one,
It's your heart.
I'm all about your heart,
Not about the gifts you bring.
I don't want your lamb;
I just want you
To know I love you
And want you to respond
With your whole heart.
It's the best offering ever
And will never
Be rejected.

NOTE TO SELF
Broken hearts make the best gifts.

TAILSPIN

"If you do not do what is right, sin is crouching at your door;
it desires to have you, but you must rule over it."

—Genesis 4:7

In counseling for months, one woman consistently failed to act responsibly for herself and her small children. Because of her passivity, she'll lose her apartment. She and her children will live in their car if she doesn't choose differently. She is in a personal death spiral of sorts, dependent on others to make decisions for her and take care of her family.

Forbes defined death spiral states (or governmental regions) as those with a greater percentage of "takers" (people paid by the government through employment, pension, or welfare) than "makers" (those working in the private sector). The second factor that determined whether a state spiraled toward death concerned the state's fiscal status: "large debts, an uncompetitive business climate, weak home prices, and bad trends in employment."[1]

This isn't new news, really, although *Forbes* thought so. Haven't we been in what the article's writer, William Baldwin, called a "fiscal tailspin" ever since Eden foreclosed?

We've inherited from Adam, Eve, and their children the soul disorder called Following Your Impulse. In spite of eating from the Tree of Knowledge of Good and Evil, we seem unable to choose the good side of that with natural casualness. Evil beckons, the bakery smell piped outside the storefront. Come, eat, taste, try.

It doesn't have to appear overtly evil. The mother I mentioned earlier isn't sinning with panache—she's not raging, in a haze of drugs, or in a torrid affair. But not choosing to act positively has thrown her in a tailspin. She's now caught in the eddy. Tailspin sin.

We're all in a fiscal tailspin. We dwell in the debt caused by sin, by its outworkings of violence, ugliness, hatred, loneliness, depression, abandonment, poverty, war, and greed. We think, though, that one bite won't hurt us.

But it will. Desire frays the optic nerve of our soul, leaving us short-sighted and self-focused, if not entirely sightless. For the woman facing homelessness, the problem wasn't the outward circumstances. Nor is it for us, most likely. We have within ourselves the power to destroy ourselves. Desire draws us to self-destruction.

Every day, we engage in a life-or-death battle. We don't recognize the battle lines, but God was clear when Cain moped outside Eden's doorjamb. "If you do what is right, will you not be accepted? But if you do not do what is right, sin is crouching at your door; it desires to have you, but you must rule over it" (Gen. 4:7).

As we try to find our way out of tailspin sin and the eddies of poor choices, we can rely on the principle God fleshed out for Cain. Recognizing what is right is probably the single most critical step. We give in to impulse because we don't stop to ask ourselves: Is this right? What does God say about this? What will happen if I follow this path, this impulse?

If we don't identify and question the impulse and the feeling behind it, we will almost always make a mess of our next step.

This identification process takes practice. How much easier to stop fighting the eddy. But Jesus would tell us, many years after Cain succumbed, "Watch and pray so that you will not fall into temptation. The spirit is willing, but the flesh is weak" (Matt. 26:41). Cain proved the latter. Following Jesus' technique, we can prove the former: Watch and pray. And the guarantee: You will not fall into temptation.

The Enemy won't win.

TRAVELING MERCY
Dear one,
Tailspin sin,
Your death spiral
Stops here:
Recognize,
Watch,
Pray.
Sin waits,
But you can master it
With my help.

NOTE TO SELF
Recognize, watch, pray.

NOTE
1. William Baldwin, "Do You Live in a Death Spiral State?" *Forbes*, November 25, 2012, accessed March 31 2015, http://www.forbes.com/sites/baldwin/2012/11/25/do-you-live-in-a-death-spiral-state.

SOUL OIL SPILL

"If you do what is right, will you not be accepted?"

—GENESIS 4:7

Who but God could foresee the effects of Eden's loss that spill into our lives today?[1] In 2010, months after the well in the Gulf of Mexico spewed 206 million gallons of oil into the waters, killing eleven workers and untold quantities of sea life, and putting generations-old businesses out of business, an emergency plug finally sealed the hole. Experts viewing the surface of the waters declared a triumphant "All clean." They declared most of the damage contained, with micro-eaters under the water to thank. Absolutely magical results to the naked eye.

On the surface at least. But beneath those waters, far beneath, layers of oil sank to the bottom of the Gulf of Mexico and continued to contaminate the living salt waters and pollute and destroy marine life. The long-term damage is incalculable. Sounds like Eden's consequences to me. Like Cain spilling Abel's blood and then denying any responsibility for his brother.

So often, too often, we view our lives spiritually in this way. We spew (if we are honest) before we come to know

God, then Christ enters our lives, contains us, and cleans us up. We declare to the world, on the surface, "All clean." At church, everyone sure seems all clean. No problems, everybody just happy all the time.

Have we reduced Jesus, cheapened him, to magician status, using tricks and mirrors to fix our broken gasket and gushing well?

What a surprise, then, when someone from our pew spews, spiritually or emotionally speaking. Perhaps hurt turns to anger then rage, especially when buried beneath the "all clean" waters of Christian living. Maybe an affair, addiction, abuse. When *we* spew, there is more than surprise. We feel guilt, if we're honest (there's that word again), but beneath that, shame coats our souls, that lurking layer of contamination that says, "You are bad. You are not good enough. You are a mistake." Incalculable damage.

Maybe it's not even spewing. Maybe it's a bubble of anger or irritation or distancing a little too frequently, or a less noticeable or more forgivable sin. Impatience, perhaps. Or saying yes to everything for all the wrong reasons.

God knows the oil blanketing the bottom of the Gulf and the oil spill sinking in our souls. When wounds erupt, hurting others, it's called sin. Plain old sin. Big, little, it all separates us from God and others. A costly cover up, day after week after year.

While time might allow the micro-eaters to digest some of the pollution in the Gulf, though I doubt this, it doesn't work that way for us spiritually. Instead, the oil eats away at our insides until eventually it breaks through to the outside world. What if instead of a pretend "all clean" diagnosis, we dive down deep and measure the oil spill that lines our hearts? What if we come clean with someone? Ourselves for starters, then God, then someone else? What if we hold a community dive, then break the surface of the water with the "oil" in a container and put it on the altar at church?

What if we actually believed James' words: "Confess your sins to each other, and pray for each other so that you might be healed" (James 5:16)? Imagine the cleansing movement that would begin sweeping the deep layers of our damaged world, the wounded and weary people outside the walls who still dog-paddle ahead, smiling through pain so intense they feel a thousand or ten thousand leagues under the sea with no oxygen.

Imagine, then, the "all clean" rejoicing at that altar and in the hallways of heaven.

Today, I'm starting my diving regimine. And you know what they say: "Don't swim alone." So I hope you'll come along.

TRAVELING MERCY
Dear one,
Dive deep
Together,
And we'll search out
The oil spill.
Community dives
Are good for the world,
So share,
Confess,
Pray.
And then you really will sound
The "All clean."
The world waits.

NOTE TO SELF
Organize community dive.

NOTE
1. A portion of this devotion appeared as: Jane Rubietta, "Soul Oil Spill," *indeed* Magazine, May/June 2011, 9–10.

FEBRUARY DEVOTIONS

FEBRUARY 1

A SHEPHERD'S LIFE AND DEATH AND LIFE

He will stand and shepherd his flock in the strength
of the LORD. . . . And they will live securely, for then
his greatness will reach to the ends of the earth.

—MICAH 5:4

Abel, the first shepherd, brought the firstborn of his sheep, the fattest and best he had to give from his entire flock. For all we know, Cain may have brought the best grain. But God looked past the offering to the offerer's heart, a heart that soon would binge on evil. God looked and found favor instead with Abel's offering, one given from an upright heart.

Abel the shepherd, killed by a jealous brother whose shame and anger over his own inadequacies drove him to murder.

We know so little about Abel, beyond these Scriptures. His blood cried out from the ground, God said. Otherwise, we hear nothing about him in new detail until thousands of years later. The One called Messiah would speak of the blood of the prophets, beginning with Abel (see Luke 11:50–51).

Abel, a prophet? Prophets look toward the future and declare something about it, about God's presence in the future. Abel, the shepherd, whose full-hearted offering got him killed, pointed ahead. One day, the Messiah would appear and proclaim, "I am the good shepherd" (John 10:11). The Good Shepherd, who would present a perfect offering. He would lay down his life for his sheep.

The first shepherd brought his heart with his offering. He was killed for it. And so it was with Jesus, the Great Shepherd of the sheep, who offered a pleasing and perfect sacrifice, completely sufficient because it was given from an entirely pure heart and a perfect life.

Though Abel didn't willingly lay down his life, Christ did. Though both were murdered, Christ knew before donning flesh and blood that he would be giving his life. He chose to live, and he chose to die.

Unlike Abel's death, though, Christ's death would not be permanent. Rather, his death and resurrection would conquer and cancel death for all time.

Not only was Abel a prophet, according to Jesus, but when Jesus mentioned this second-born son of Adam and Eve, he said, "the blood of righteous Abel" (Matt. 23:35). *Righteous*, a powerful term to describe Abel's right standing before God. With Jesus' descriptor for Abel comes the first mention of a righteous person in the Scriptures—words spoken by the One who called the world into existence with his very word. Jesus should know.

The writer of the letter to the Hebrews offered this powerful hope and purpose in the midst of a world of death and dying: The blood of righteous Abel still cries from the ground, but the ground could not keep Jesus. "The God of peace, who through the blood of the eternal covenant brought back from the dead our Lord Jesus, that great Shepherd of the sheep [and will] equip you with everything good for doing his will, and may he work in us what is pleasing to him, through Jesus Christ" (Heb. 13:20–21).

Two shepherds pointing us to a new day. Abel's life and death. Christ's life and death, and life offering us peace and hope and equipping us with everything we need for God's work. Though our offerings are always insufficient, our hearts are righteous because of Christ, the great Good Shepherd. The perfect offering. The perfect purpose.

TRAVELING MERCY
Dear one,
The great Good Shepherd
Rose from the dead
And now fully equips you
To live this life
With peace
In the midst of death,
With everything you need.
My heart is pleased with you
And will work what is pleasing
In you
And through you in this world.
Peace to you.
And purpose, too.

NOTE TO SELF
My life and heart, the perfect offering.

YOUR BEST SELF

"I will be hidden from your presence;
I will be a restless wanderer on the earth."

—Genesis 4:14

In the movie *Wild*, Cheryl Strayed says that it took her a lifetime to become who her mother believed her to be. To become her best self. Her grief and loss and the wounds sustained on the journey masked themselves in high-risk behavior. Her path dragged her through destructive habits and relationships, all attempts to combat her feelings of abandonment. In the process, she abandoned herself, her own legitimate longings for love and her conviction about right and wrong. She was, like Cain, a restless wanderer on the earth.

Finding our way has become a hike on an unmarked and unrated trail. Unexpected drop-offs and path obstructions create a frightening journey. En route from Eden to today, we abandon ourselves to a sad and brokenhearted (and backward) approach to combatting abandonment.

Maybe it's addictive behavior. Or we abandon ourselves in church-applauded ways, certain others' gifts and talents take precedence over our own. That their needs are more important, their ideas and insights brighter than ours.

We abandon ourselves, trying to disappear through under-performing or overachieving. We become what others need or believe us to be. Sometimes we abandon ourselves through rebellion or flagrant attempts to be noticed, since even negative notice is better than none at all.

In this confusion, many of us feel powerless to change. But we no longer need to follow this script. Yes, Eden is behind us. Sure, we've been abandoned by people who should have loved us better; we've been let down in small and colossal ways. But abandonment doesn't own us; it is no longer the truth about us.

In spite of Christian teaching to the contrary, we can't confuse self-care and self-recognition with self-centered behavior. Pretending we have no needs hurts us and our people. It damages the unique path God wants to cut for us through this earthly journey. It also is a flat-out denial of the gifts and personality God gave us, and of God's calling for us to be a blessing in this world.

Establishing and observing personal boundaries help stop self-defeating self-abandonment. If I can separate myself from others and expect that I will be a different person with a different approach than they, I begin to set boundaries. Sometimes I have to say to myself, "Wait. That's what someone else thinks. What do *you* think?" Or, "What is my response rather than my reaction here?"

In a time of lostness or off-road trekking, instead of dwelling in a place of confusion or exhaustion, try asking, "What do I need right now?" Maybe it's food, sleep, movement, conversation, a hug. In noticing, we honor the way God made us and the needs that come with our particular package.

Other times, when I feel hidden from God's presence or fret that my plodding life doesn't look remotely like the path that someone else bounds along, I remember: "I will lead the blind by ways they have not known, along unfamiliar paths I will guide them; I will turn the darkness into light before them and make the rough places smooth. These are the things I will do; I will not forsake them" (Isa. 42:16). We will find ourselves, we will find God, and we will find our path, if we remember.

TRAVELING MERCY

Dear one,
You've lost Eden.
You've even lost yourself sometimes.
But you haven't lost me.
And I sure haven't lost you
Or lost sight of you.
Remember how I created you?
I would never abandon
The work of my hands.
That's you,
And nothing can snatch you
From my hands.
So hold tightly to me,
And you'll begin to be your best self
Ever.
No more abandonment.

NOTE TO SELF

Hold hands when crossing the street. Or the world.

ON THE WAY HOME

"I will be a restless wanderer on the earth."

—GENESIS 4:14

We are people on the way, people trying to find their way. I bet we have more maps and apps today than all the maps in the world combined up until this time. And we need them to find our way—except they don't answer the critical question, "Where are we going?" Nor do they address the issue, "How do we get there?"

Not every path leads home, unless you count the long way. But every path teaches us something directional, if we stop to ask. What have we learned on *this* detour? What would we do differently if we came to that juncture again? Would we change anything? What about this leg of the trip has changed us, our attitudes, our hearts, or our minds? How about our relationships or our approaches to a specific relationship?

Imagine the confusion outside Eden. Adam and Eve burst through the gates and land in a world without roads, without wayside rest stations, and without signs saying, "This way, thirty-six miles to your new home."

They didn't have to pay rent or utilities, so in that respect their cost of living was pretty low. In other ways, it was exceptionally high. It had cost them Eden, and now they would be constantly on the road to somewhere. A part of their heart, and ours as well, would always be set like our map app, with "home" as that ethereal, untrackable, Eden. That place of safety, of perfect love, of incandescent light.

This is one of the gifts since Eden: There is a little computer chip in our heart that says, "Find home." That tiny tracking device alerts us by messages of discontentment or disappointment, or of distress or discouragement. "Not home. Keep looking." It beeps its little infrared probe and says, "This isn't your home." We look at someone else as home, and the Taser of longing hits our nerve. "Nope. Not home." We glance a little too long or longingly at a handsome or beautiful stranger, a hot car, or a gorgeous home, and the sensor inside buzzes. "Wrong answer. Not home." These become our signposts, telling us where not to turn and when to refuse off-roading.

If we listen to the warning bells and clangs, if we tune in to the descant of longing in the deepest part of our soul, we will know, like Adam and Eve, that home is somewhere, but it is intangible. It is not numbers on a fence post, a mailbox to call our own, and a big welcome mat at the front door. Not keys to the late-model car or the corner office.

Rather, home is that place where we are perfectly loved, described by words like *unfailing*, *forever*, *everlasting*, *faithful*, *forgiving*, *steadfast*, and *new every morning*. Home is where God is. Wherever God dwells, we find our home. This is the heartbreak of Eden. And this is the good news in which we now live: Our God has come to earth in Emmanuel, God with us, and we have our forever home. Jesus told us, after all, "I go to prepare a place for you" (John 14:2 NASB).

We can reset our app.

TRAVELING MERCY
Dear one,
Home is wherever I am
And you with me.
Where you live
Is irrelevant.
Find your home
In me.
I am your greatest love
And your safest place
And your best adventure
Ever.

NOTE TO SELF
Reset app all day long.

ADDING UP

So Cain went out from the LORD's presence and lived
in the land of Nod, east of Eden.

—GENESIS 4:16

If Eve didn't have postpartum depression after giving birth to those two boys, how on earth did she navigate the dark abyss of life after Abel's murder? It must be the worst PPD ever, the grief of being parted forever from your child.

Her loss was long-term, and it was even bigger than simply the death of Abel, as overwhelming as that was. She also lost her other son, Cain, to his anger and his lack of repentance. (You'll remember that he denied knowing anything about his brother, and even asked, "Am I my brother's keeper?" Cain wasn't sorry he'd murdered his brother; he was worried about his consequence.) Eve lost Cain due to the outworkings of his sin and God's punishment: "You will be a wanderer on this earth." No "home for the holiday" movies, no photo shoots around the Thanksgiving table, no family reunions.

Cain ran, the blight of his murder rap branded on the hide of his heart. And his mother and father, left behind, watched him run, hearts and hopes broken. They lost both their sons because of one son's crime.

We don't talk much about grief and postpartum-style depression for fathers. They don't actually give birth so they don't have that umbilical-cord attachment between mother and child. Maybe dads don't have hormone imbalance, but they definitely can become unbalanced because of the exhaustion a new baby brings, the pressures of parenting, and trying to keep a marriage together in the midst of unexpected and unexplored stress and anxiety. The role-shifting and the unknowns become a life-size jigsaw puzzle with no box-cover photo to guide its completion.

Women do not corner the market on depression, nor do they have a monopoly on the grief from a child's death. Add in the searing, doubling-over pain of murder. Then add the murderer being your firstborn son, the seed supposed to lead to the eradication of the curse. The total, rather than being simple addition, is more like exponential notation. The cloud of darkness and pain could become an impenetrable wall or shield. A weapon of mass destruction.

Adam and Eve, stripped of their awareness of God's presence, in the middle of unmitigated and irrevocable loss. No insurance plan would cover the grievous costs of broken hearts. In their world without walls, a world without any experience with loss or healing for that matter, I hope they found comfort in one another. In their shared memories of Eden, of glory, of God's presence, of happy times with their boys. In their shared grief. Because grief shared divides loneliness and multiplies healing.

And in their remembering, I hope they remembered God's promise at creation. First there was evening. And then there was morning. Light would follow the darkness of their loss.

TRAVELING MERCY
Dear one,
Share your grief
With one another.
Putting words
To pain
Helps navigate that pain
And moves you toward healing
And toward purpose.
Share your remembering,
The good and the difficult,
And my presence with you.
Joy will come
One day
In the morning.
Hearts weren't made to be broken,
But I do heal
Broken hearts.
It's in my job description.

NOTE TO SELF
Share grief and good.

FEBRUARY 5

FIRST SONG

His . . . name was Jubal; he was the father of all
who play stringed instruments and pipes.

—GENESIS 4:21

I sit in the pew, alongside our daughter and her family.
Their sweet child sits next to me, about three feet tall, her
head not even reaching to the top of the pew when we stand
to sing the hymns. She loves to sing, this beautiful child, and
can catch the notes and words and sing them a nanosecond
after she hears them.

Glancing down at the top of her shining hair, I realize that
she can't hear the words when we all stand and she is down
by our knees. She also can't see anything but the back of the
next pew, but she stands solidly and faithfully because we all
stand to worship God. My heart spills, and I squat next to her
on the floor in between the pews, holding the hymnal. She
loves to imitate other people's postures and stances, and she
squats, too. I try to compensate for her sudden shorter-ness
by lowering a bit more.

Then she about undoes me. She places her tiny hand on
my leg to steady herself and follows my words and tone. This
works for me for several notes, and then I can't see because

tears blind my eyes, and I can't sing because my throat is so clogged with overwhelming love for this tiny bone-of-my-bone child of my child's.

It is one of my holiest hushing moments, there squatting in that pew, that delicate hand resting in total trust on my knee. The perfectly pitched, piping toddler voice singing words and notes with her whole heart, even without knowing what they all mean. Although, maybe she does know what they mean, on some deep child-God-heaven-heart connection level.

What was it like for God after creation, when the first human beings opened their mouths in a song? Didn't God's heart swell to overflowing, about a million times magnified from mine that morning in church? Didn't God weep with joy, like I wept, to hear voices raised in melody, to hear the songs coming forward and rising like incense toward heaven?

And what was it like for the people when the music started to form within them and then broke through their untried vocal chords? Weren't they surprised, and didn't they have a hard time singing once they realized the beauty pouring from them, this surprising fountain of glory that somehow transported their grounded souls back to God?

Music springs forth from deep reservoirs, echoing back to the angel choruses and chorales and cantatas in heaven, all those praise and worship angels rocking and reeling and rejoicing over the creation of the universe, over the ones created "a little lower than angels" and their Creator and Maestro.

Singing. Music changes us. Softens us. Lifts us. Woos us. Encourages us. Invites us to God and to relationship. Opens our hearts to the world around us, and to eternity. Music is our response to the heavenly chorus and the unending love God offers us.

Join me in a round? It will be a real Jubal-ation.

TRAVELING MERCY
Dear one,
Music draws your heart
To mine;
And I am already
Drawn to you.
But in this place of worship
You will recognize
My deep and unending love
For you.
And music returns that love
To me.
I hear you.
I hear your voice
And your heart
And rejoice
With you.
And in you.

NOTE TO SELF
In tune or out, sing. It does the heart good.

FEBRUARY 6

"IT WAS GOOD" REPRISE

At that time people began to call on the name of the LORD.

—GENESIS 4:26

Once the couple left Eden, the scent and light and hope of that place faded but never entirely dispelled from their souls. Like a wisp of fog or the whiff of perfume trailing on a breeze—didn't they notice and remember, with a sharp and sudden pang, all that they'd lost?

And how quickly did they forget the rhythm of night and day, the security of noticing and appreciating God's presence in both the dark and light of their hours? What about the tonality of God's voice, telling them the stories of creation until the storyline was inscribed in their hearts in the cursive ink of God's love?

Didn't they hear, again, the music of the heavens in that voice? Just remembering sent chills over their skin—the glorious warmth of remembering and then fading like the sun hiding itself behind the clouds. Likely, some days they realized deeply what they'd lost, which touched a knife to their soul, as painful as a flesh wound. It was not good, not good at all.

But other days, perhaps they heard again, as though for the first time, God speaking the world into being, and then declaring: "And it was so. And it was good." Day after day, God's pronouncement of good.

When the first week rolled around in this place of dimmed glory, surely they revisited God's rhythm: "It was good. It was good. It was good." On their bad days and their not-so-bad days, maybe Adam and Eve decided to revisit God's daily words over the world.

And so can we. When the glory dims on our faith, when the pain of this world hides the sun from us and chills us to the bone, we can remember, as well: "And it was good." For those interactions with others that plunge us into despair, we can look for the "And it was good." When the stench of sin's decay fills us, we can sniff instead for the fragrance of God's presence, the "And it was good."

Making God's words personal in our lives is essential to finding our way. Otherwise the days form their own limping non-rhythm of dissatisfaction and disappointment, mingled with distress. We lose our focus and our direction because the press of discouragement shadows our eyes and covers the path of our heart.

In those places, throughout the day, at the end of the day, at the week's end, we can search out God's presence. Where is the "And it was good" for this moment? This hour or day? This week?

To do so reminds us that all is not lost. This world, while only a fraction of its former glory, is still the only place we get to live. We'll find our way forward as we find the "And it was good." See if that doesn't change the pathway of your heart and direct, and redirect, you to God.

TRAVELING MERCY
Dear one,
I saw you
And beamed.
"Wow, so good.
So very, very good,"
We said in heaven.
And now say over you
Day in and day out,
"And it was good."
Use that rhythm to restore your soul
And your perspective.
All is not lost;
I am present
In the "It was good"
And in the "It really wasn't good" moments
Of your day
And your night.

NOTE TO SELF
Find "It was good" today.

FEBRUARY 7

COUNTING THE COST

That's when men and women began praying and
worshiping in the name of God.

—Genesis 4:26 msg

A season of firsts: first earth, first people, first sin, first exile, first births, first mother, first father, first brothers, first murder, first crime scene, first burial. The dust-to-dust truth came true far too soon for this newly formed and newly wedded couple.

All those firsts. Now add in the first grief. Double the grief, triple, even. The loss of Eden. The loss of Abel through brutal murder. The loss of Cain to sin. The loss of expectancy, joy, hope. The losses would continue throughout their lifespan, and though Eve would one day exult, "God has granted me another child in place of Abel, since Cain killed him" (Gen. 4:25), children, like all human beings, are irreplaceable.

This now downwardly mobile couple lost their forever home in Eden. Adam's job was restructured and achingly redefined: work would become hard, reaping a living toil, the ground cursed with thorns and thistles. Wherever Adam and Eve set up housekeeping—whether a lean-to, a cave, or a tent—that unknown cranked up the cost of living. Childbirth, a transition of its own, would be painful—pain being yet another transition.

Finding our way in a world of changes—some of them brutal, some of them good, all of them costly in terms of our soul's responsiveness—requires attention. We must pay attention. How do we pray and worship and love God and others honestly when we haven't paid attention to where we've been and what life has meant? And most of us are so busy settling other people in the midst of their transitions and traumas, helping them find their way, that we don't even realize that our own life shifts are off the charts. But who's counting?

Not us.

Time for math class. Time to start counting. Life costs us in large and small ways. The addends of living outside of Eden in the imperfects of relationship, physical health, home, church, spiritual life, an uncertain future—the sum of these is far more than their individual parts. So for our own sakes, and for the sake of the people we love—for the sake of the God we serve—we need to consider their costs on us. The toll on our souls is substantial.

Try itemizing your personal life shifts, as we did for Adam and Eve. Now include the changes in the lives of people you love, because honestly, if they're in flux and we care about them at all, their changes affect us. How have these shifts hurt you? Your relationships? What about your heart, your trust levels, and your life with God?

We will find our way, and yes, it will be through pain. But as we tally the costs of that pain and recognize how it impacts us, we will move toward our purpose. Every single experience in our lives informs our faith, teaches us about God, and provides a commonality for reaching others with the hope that we find, in this, the God of all the earth.

Pain is, after all, one of our greatest common denominators. When we call on the name of the Lord, processing our own pain, we begin to love others in new ways, with new grace, out of the reservoir of God's comfort.

What better purpose could we possibly seek?

TRAVELING MERCY
Dear one,
Life is costly,
But I have the means
To help you move from pain
To purpose.
How do you find your way
If you don't know where you've been,
Don't know what it's cost you,
Don't know how I've been
Present to you en route?
I promise
This will lead to prayer and worship
And to healing and hope
And to good words to offer others
Who've lost their way
On this painful journey.

NOTE TO SELF
Process pain. Find purpose.

JOURNEY TO REST

"This one will bring us comfort from our labor and
from the painful toil of our hands."

GENESIS 5:29 NET

As God predicted, sin crouched at Cain's door, but rather
than master it, Cain succumbed to the desire for authority and
control, rising up against Abel in murder. Genesis 4:8–11
repeats *brother* six times, emphasizing Cain's brutal crime—
your brother, Cain, your *brother*. There's a huge difference
between "cleaving" and "cleaver," Cain.

To Cain, who worked the ground, whose brother's blood
cried out from that very ground, God said, "Now you are
under a curse and driven from the ground." Then God cursed
the ground: "It will no longer yield its crops for you." Bad
news for a field man, forcing Cain to keep traveling to find
suitable land.

Cain, decrying his punishment (but not repenting of his
manslaughter), hollered to God, "No fair! I will be hidden
from your presence."

But God said nothing about hiding from Cain. Rather, Cain
"went out from the presence of the LORD." He removed himself
from God. God marked him with a sign of protection, promising

that if anyone killed him, "Cain will be avenged seven times as much" (4:15–16 NET).

Cain ran eastward, landing in the land of Nod, which means, fittingly, "wander." He set to building a city, since farming would be futile, like tilling limestone, though a city for a wanderer seems counterintuitive. Maybe it speaks of his longing for home.

Adam's firstborn named the city after his own firstborn, Enoch. The family line expanded. Grandson Lamech instituted polygamy then gloated over spilling blood. Because farming wasn't part of the family's future, his sons, whose names sound like either bad poetry or a bad joke—Jabal, Jubal, and Tubal-Cain—are credited with the beginnings of tent-keeping, the arts, and metalworking. All told, a rather breathless recitation in Genesis 4:17–24.

Genesis 5 recounts the genealogy of Adam. Adam and Eve had Seth, Abel's "replacement," when people begin to call on the name of the Lord. Adam, the Scriptures say, "fathered a son in his own likeness, according to his image" (5:3). And we witness the decay resulting from this shift from God's image to Adam's.

The similarity in names between Cain's descendants and Seth's could cause some confusion, but Seth's grandson Enoch walked with God and then wasn't, because God took him to heaven. He is one of the few people to never see death in Scripture. His son Methuselah holds the record of the longest life: 969 years. Even so, the chorus of "and he died" includes him, leaving us with "and he died" repeated nine times in Genesis 5.

With the bright exception of Enoch, the family line of Adam tasted only death. The world twirled into a desperate dance with evil. Throughout all of this, God's voice in history was silent, painfully silent. Until we reach Noah.

Noah, son of Adam, son of Seth, son of Lamech. Noah, a name to live up to, because "this one will bring us comfort from our labor and from the painful toil of our hands" (Gen. 5:29 NET).

Noah. Rest. After a break-neck departure from Eden and the full-tilt race to pain and evil, we reach Noah. A tumultuous route to rest but worth the Dramamine. For Noah leads us to the One who says, "Come to me, all you who are weary and burdened, and I will give you rest" (Matt. 11:28). Just as Lamech, son of Seth, son of Adam, hoped.

TRAVELING MERCY
Dear one,
The dance with evil
Continues through the years.
But no more
Must evil
Be your dance partner.
Come to me,
Find rest for your soul,
Lay down your load
Of sorrow and pain,
Give up your sin—
It's all too heavy in your boat—
And rest, now.
Just rest.

NOTE TO SELF
Lighten the load, learn to lie down.

GIANTS FOR GOD

Nephilim were on the earth in those days—and also
afterward. . . . They were the heroes of old, men of renown.

—Genesis 6:4

Some translations call these giants, the Nephilim, heroes or
men of renown. *The Stone's Edition of the Chumash* casts these
big guys in a very unfavorable light: "They were the mighty
of old, men of devastation."[1] In other words, they were big and
strong and did a lot of damage. Context can almost always
generate a light bright enough to clear up interpretive controversy.
How can a nice group of guys be mentioned in a paragraph
that explains God's anger and justifies the flood?

In addition to the Nephilim's mention, we know from later
Scriptures that some exceptionally tall people really existed and
became famous (for example, Og, king of Bashan, mentioned
in Deut. 3:11). Just a century ago, a true giant of a man,
Patrick O'Brien of Cork, Ireland, died, with his skeleton now
on display at the Royal College of Surgeons.

Research on his remains showed that a pituitary gland
producing too much growth hormone may have enlarged the
skull at the base of the brain. Sometimes a pituitary tumor
causes this bone thickening. If the disorder begins in childhood,

arms and legs grow faster than normal. Both Patrick O'Brien and Hen-Nekht, an Egyptian nobleman who lived a millennium before Og of Bashan, had this enlargement. In fact, most of the giants whose bones have been examined have a similar aberration. There's a good chance that there really were giants in the land (see Num. 13), who were the ancestors of Mr. O'Brien and Hen-Nekht.

So whether they existed is not really up for debate. But here's the question: Were these great big men of old actually great men?

Research shows that height is an advantage in our world. Tall people tend to enjoy higher socioeconomic status, better jobs, more attractive mates, and general adulation.

When I shopped recently, a white-haired woman hunched over her cart and beamed up at me. "You're so tall," she said.

Well, she certainly was astute. Except, my height is hard to miss. But it is also not remarkable. Minutes later, she circled back around the store, her chin nearly level with her cart's handle, and found me again. "You really *are* tall," as though to confirm that she could trust her perception. Again, "tall people" are in some ways revered and seen as special for no particularly good reason. I have no control over the length of my bones.

The giants of Genesis were among those without a boarding pass to enter the ark. These big humans are mentioned in the same breath as those whose thoughts were only evil and whose deeds were only violent. Rather than the Nephilim's height, their taking advantage of others, perhaps among other things, was what was reprehensible. Otherwise, maybe they would've been called to be oarsmen aboard the ark.

Regardless of height, what makes us people of renown versus devastation? Genesis 6:9 touches on this. "Noah was a righteous man, blameless among the people of his time, and he walked faithfully with God." He might not have been respected by his peers, but he was a giant for God.

The tall and short of it? Be a person who walks with God and you will do what is right and be remembered. You may be short, but if you walk with God, your heart will be enlarged. Then you will certainly be a gigantic force of good among God's people. And in this world.[2]

TRAVELING MERCY
Dear one,
Regardless of your width or height
What matters to me is the size of your heart
And shape of it.
Walking, I might add, is good for both.
Be a giant force for me,
For good,
For hope
In this world
As you walk this land.
Do you have your walking shoes?

NOTE TO SELF
Practice walking tall.

NOTES
1. Rabbi Nosson Scherman, *The Chumash: The Stone Edition with Complete Sabbath Prayers* (Brooklyn, NY: Mesorah Publications, 2000), 27.

2. Giant thanks to my husband, Rich, who wrestled with the research on the Nephilim.

FINDING WHOSE WAY?

Woe to them! They have taken the way of Cain.

—JUDE 11

The way of Cain? As in, shame leading to jealousy, anger, depression, blame, murder, blame-shifting, and responsibility-avoiding. All leading to the curse of never being able to settle down (see Gen. 4:1–16). Ever. A restless wanderer on the earth.

Cain's anger—literally, "he felt hot with, burned with, anger"—resulted from the shaming sense of not measuring up. Cain felt rejected.

Note the progression: not measuring up, feeling judged, hot with anger, sin. Even though God addressed this with Cain, Cain couldn't receive the truth and learn from it. Instead, shame simmered, reshaping itself into vengeance in the cauldron of anger.

Cain heard God's correction and guidance (see 4:7) as judgment and rejection, though that isn't in the text. But shame will do that to us all.

Outside of Eden, judgment would become one of our greatest fears and greatest temptations. We would interpret someone's unfavorable response to the works of our hands as their judgment of our worth. Then, without recognizing this, we react out of our lack of self-awareness.

"Why are you angry? Why is your face downcast?" God asked Cain. Good questions. In other words, shovel to the bottom of the emotional sinkhole. Otherwise, emotions' power traps us. By identifying the "sin crouching outside," we'll find our way with far less calamity and fallout from our pain and sin.

Cain was cursed to wander because he let his inadequacies prompt his actions. We, too, are tempted with the lies: We will never measure up, never be good enough, always be inferior, so keep moving and we won't have to try. Be angry, blame, attack, run.

Trying to outrun your own footprints is exhausting. Outrunning your sin impossible. Cain's murder of his brother didn't lead to repentance, but to a lifelong marathon of avoidance. Anger, intended as a tool that converts, instead contorted him into an angry man who raised an angry son, and more angry generations followed.

Anger unattended will destroy. But if we dare to invite God to help us uncover its deep roots while we wear the gardening gloves of God's grace, we'll begin to heal. We'll start to act, not out of our brokenness, but out of our forgiven- and accepted-ness.

This appears to be possible. Fast forward a few generations to Noah. Genesis 6:8 reads, "Noah found favor in the eyes of the LORD."

Take a deep breath here. Isn't that our real hope, finding favor with God?

The word *favor* in the original language means "stooped, condescension, moving to a lower level." God bent down, in other words, and bestowed kindness on Noah.

So much of our life's energy and attention is spent trying to find and win favor. That lack of favor results in workaholism, competition, jealousy, inferiority, and serial attaching to and detaching from others. Or, what happened with Cain, whose feelings of disfavor ultimately propelled him to murder.

So why God's favor for Noah? We learn three things about him in 6:9. In contrast to the way of Cain wandering away from God, Noah walked with God—a phrase used elsewhere that means "rubbing elbows, living and working in close proximity with God."

Further, Noah was a righteous man, an amazing description when the first seven verses of chapter 6 detail the world's violence and evil, and God's heartbreak.

Noah was blameless among his contemporaries. Blameless doesn't mean perfect—rather, mature, fully formed. We aren't talking about a sinless man, but a man of integrity—wholeness, all parts agreeing. It's a statement of spiritual and emotional cohesiveness.

When people saw Noah, they saw God in and through him.

Cain ran from God. Noah walked with God. Our heart can choose what our legs will do.

TRAVELING MERCY

Dear one,
Choose your path—
Whether you'll run away
Or walk with me.
The way of Cain
Or the way of Noah.
Before you react,
Let's be clear:
Pay attention to your emotions.
Bring them to me,
So they become a tool that shapes you
For the path you'll walk.
You'll look more like me.
I promise.

NOTE TO SELF

Listen to your heart. Choose wholeness.

FLOTATION DEVICE

By faith Noah, when warned about things not yet seen, in holy fear
built an ark to save his family. By his faith he condemned the world
and became heir of the righteousness that is in keeping with faith.

—HEBREWS 11:7

In the beginning. Such glory in the world. Angels singing,
360-degree beauty. The transformation from formlessness
and void complete, and completely wonderful. God couldn't
have been more pleased. It was good, good, good.

So far, everything in creation represented relatively low
risk. So far, all of creation would live and grow by instinct rather
than personal will or choice. But on the sixth day, right after
creating all the animals, God noticed. Something was missing
from all the glory. Nothing looked like God in all creation. And
so God said, "Let us make man in our image."

It was a calculated risk. Giving people the power of
thought, the ability and freedom to choose—well, God would
take that chance. He would throw it all on the table for this
spin of the creation wheel. It would be worth it, because at
this rate, everything was just good. But after God molded the
first man from the dirt, still, creation lacked something. Then
from the man's rib, God performed the first bone transplant
and fashioned a woman.

Finally God pronounced creation, "Very good!" Fabulous, wonderful, the pinnacle. Heavenly high fives all around.

After the first sin, after the free fall in Eden and the exile, humanity swirled down in an endless twist of evil. Abel's murder, Cain's malicious family line—malware in the system. But hope spoke up with Seth's birth. People began to call on the name of the Lord.

At least, perhaps, Seth's people did. The rest of the people on earth plunged into such evil they were unrecognizable from Adam and Eve and the glory of the first couple. Every thought evil. The heart desperately evil. Evil everywhere.

Brokenhearted and mourning the fall of the finest of creation, God regretted making people—they bore no resemblance to "human." It was the bleakest day in history. God's heart was deeply troubled.

The writer of Genesis uses sweeping and inclusive words: "The LORD saw . . . that *every* inclination of the thoughts of the human heart was *only* evil *all* the time" (6:5, emphasis added). With these universal descriptors, this is a level of evil that we can't imagine, even in the worst horror movies, even on the worst news round-ups from around the world.

Except for one glimmer on the soon-to-disappear horizon. Lamech, great-grandson of Seth, had a son named Noah, who was righteous, blameless among the people. Optimistically, his name meant "rest," and Lamech hoped Noah would reverse the curse on the ground and give them rest.

How Lamech envisioned this, we'll never know; he died before experiencing the rest he'd sought. Noah, however, wasn't due to rest anytime soon. Sometime before his six hundredth birthday, Noah heard from God about building an ark, about one and half times as big as a football field. That's a lot of boat, especially one to be built during the pre-nail stage of the construction industry, before saw mills and rotating blades. A lot of trees to fell, hand hewing, work, work, work, and no rest.

It was more than a lot of boat. It was a lot of desperation and heartache. But Noah's faithfulness would result in the literal salvation of humanity. What do we do with a God who would wipe out all of humanity? Correct ourselves: God saved one, who saved seven, who would in the long run lead to the One who would save you. And me. And the human race. That One would be our resting place.

TRAVELING MERCY
Dear one,
A lot of boat
And a lot of hope
Went into that giant flotation device.
Today you get a free start-over,
And tomorrow too.
No more boat.
That ship has sailed and docked,
And now you have a new Captain
Of your faith.
What do you say?
All aboard?

NOTE TO SELF
Like Noah, offer safe passage to others.

HONEY-DO

Noah did everything just as God commanded him.
—GENESIS 6:22

Fifteen hours of asphalt left.[1] Green occasionally lined the roadsides. Sometimes hills. But mostly, I was in brown, dull flatland. My mind focused on nothing more intense or thought-provoking or deep than the speedometer, the lines on the road, and the gratings on the pavement indicating I'd gone off the edge. I just wanted to get home.

In a moment of guilt, or perhaps conviction, I noticed my brainlessness and thought, "I should pray rather than drive around without a sentence in my head." This seemed good, and efficient. There's never a shortage of people and circumstances to pray for, and a chronic shortage of praying time. At least, this is what I tell myself.

So I began. "Dear God, please . . ."

I stopped, chastened. I meant to race through my list, A to Z. To cover everyone I knew, loved, worried about; every circumstance I could remember, every woman from a recent conference, every upcoming event. The list. We all have them and add to them regularly. A friend in need. Someone on the prayer concerns list at church. An issue in government or on the news. On the list.

Prayer lists remind us that the world is bigger than our personal concerns, that the world of people and problems needs prayer. I like lists, a lot.

That day, I did a Mario Andretti into the throne room, like Hebrews 4:16 bids us, but forgot I approached the King, the One in charge of all the people on my list. I stormed the castle and started in with all the needs and demands, issuing God orders. Bless her, heal that relationship, give him a job, help that health problem. What an assumption: I know what is best for these people I love.

Our refrigerator door sports a honeydew-colored, melon-shaped pad. Beneath the clever header, "Honey Do List," lines run down the page, ready to fill with the endless listing of tasks to be accomplished. Usually I load it with grocery needs. I have my own endless to-do lists, and reject the idea of inflicting my own agenda on family members who might possibly be immersed in their own list of projects.

Genesis 6:22 says, "Noah did everything just as God commanded him." But I'd created a honey-do list for God, a reverse God-to-Noah memo. A whole long litany of manipulations and machinations for the Lord of heaven and earth to tend. The great fix-it guy in the sky. A cosmic handyman waiting for orders.

How presumptuous. Who am I to tell God what to do? The Scriptures bid us to pray without ceasing (1 Thess. 5:17). I'm not sure they mean, though, to constantly throw a list at God. I'm missing a significant part of the prayer package: relationship. After all, this is why I don't put a list on the fridge for people to tend. It doesn't feel relational.

So instead of rolling out heavenly honey-dos, gripping the steering wheel and keeping the pedal halfway to the metal, try this: "Dear God . . ." And breathe. Then mentally hold the person to God. And wait, staying still in God's presence. Then, maybe a thousand dotted lines later, another person. Just wait behind the wheel in relationship with the God of all the earth.

Do I finish my list? Doubtful. Sometimes I should just lay it down, saying, "You know, Lord, you alone know." Sometimes I just keep driving, fixing my mind on Jesus, and head for home.

TRAVELING MERCY
Dear one,
The best honey-do list includes,
But is not limited to,
"Come to me,"
"Seek me,"
"Follow me."
You'll find your way
As you track after obedience.
And I will watch the comings and goings
For you and those you love.
And you know that I know.

NOTE TO SELF
"Trust" and "Wait" are prayer postures, too.

NOTE
1. A version of this devotion was printed as: Jane Rubietta, "Honey-Do," *indeed* Magazine, September/October 2012, 2–3.

VIEW FROM THE MEDIAN

The waters flooded the earth for a hundred and fifty days.

—GENESIS 7:24

We all felt like Noah with the rain.[1] Solid walls of rain. But tonight the highway was clear, the celestial spigot turned off at last. All I wanted was to get home from this latest retreat as fast as was legal. Calculating the time, I phoned my husband and told him: 11 p.m. ETA.

Suddenly, a snake of red glowed in front of me. I slammed to a halt, craning to see the problem. How long had these semis and cars been waiting? I jiggled my foot in anxiety. Scheduling had taken me from one ministry event to the next without downtime, so I had given up a rare, free night in a deluxe suite with an in-room Jacuzzi to zoom home.

Now this. I groaned and thumped the steering wheel with my palm. I fiddled with radio knobs for a station with news of an interstate problem. Nothing.

A car in front of me broke out of line, roared across the median, and sped in the opposite direction. Then another. I perked up. I could do that. But how would I reroute? I didn't know the area, didn't have a GPS, and had no Internet package on my cell.

But the other cars and pickup trucks made their escape. I pulled onto the left shoulder. After looking both ways, I crept into the patch between the roads. When it cleared, I punched the accelerator. Mud spun from the wheels, the car sank. More gas. More mud. More stuck.

I got out of the car to ask for help. Mud sucked around my ankles. A kind semi-truck driver tried to push me out and gave up. Another driver shoved. Nothing. No budging this car.

Ticked at my idiocy, I called my husband. I had been trying to get home to *him*. Rich is the embodiment of 1 Corinthians 13: love is patient, kind, bears all things, etc. Without any shaming words for my predicament, he located a towing company.

Meanwhile, I sulked, sunk in the mud. Then I remembered I was nearly out of gas and switched off the ignition. The bottleneck of traffic on the homeward side of the interstate cleared, and traffic flowed past in a stream. I fumed.

My mind shifted to the retreat and the women I'd met: A former anorexic. A woman who still is. A third eating disorder. A wife tired of living. Another reliving sexual abuse from her past. A woman grieving her infertility. Another scared about moving into a church plant with an instable marriage. My heart hurt at their stories, at their pain, at the fear behind them all. Talk about mud outside the ark.

As I sat parked in my car in the thick dark night, I wondered: Why hadn't I just waited on the interstate like the rest of the traffic? The problem is the not knowing—choosing to sit for an unknown length of time, possibly hours (been there, done that, another story) when there might be a way to avoid it. And isn't fear based on the not knowing?

But the unknown greets us at every turn. I thought I'd chosen the lesser unknown, and followed the lemming law. Except all the other cars made it through, and I got mired.

There's nothing like the vantage point of the median, and perhaps that's what the retreat was: a median on life's interstate, a temporary stopping point from the fast lane to refocus, to pray, to cry out for help, to consider the journey. A place to recognize our needs, to humbly wait. To flash our hazard lights.

And to know that though we don't know the path ahead of us, we know the God of the path. And one way or another, that tow truck will be along. Shortly. Or eventually. But along.

TRAVELING MERCY
Dear one,
A median will do just fine—
A place to wait,
To examine,
To trust me
A little bit bigger.
I have you covered
And will tow you out
And lead you forward.
Just waiting
For the right time.

NOTE TO SELF
Use the current median wisely.

NOTE
1. A version of this devotion was printed as: Jane Rubietta, "View from the Median," *indeed* Magazine, January/February 2012, 15–16.

FEBRUARY 14

FLOODWATERS

But God remembered Noah and all the wild animals
and livestock that were with him in the ark.

—GENESIS 8:1

"Heaven came down and glory filled my soul," exults the 1961 hymn. The heavens sure appeared to come down on Noah, a deluge of heaven. Evidently Noah experienced the first rains ever, based on Genesis 2:5–6. "The LORD God had not sent rain on the earth . . . but streams came up from the earth and watered the whole surface of the ground."

The doors of the ark closed and God sealed in Noah and his family and the enormous sampling of living creatures from the earth. Then the rains came. The floodgates of heaven opened like an endless dam had burst.

"The waters flooded the earth for a hundred and fifty days" (7:24). Five months is a long time to float without land in sight. Forty days and nights is an eternity to watch curtains of rain fall and to feel the ark rock and rise as the waters increased. Gray days, long unlit days blending into long soul-dark nights. Seasick and heartsick are not a good combination. Throw in a little Seasonal Affective Disorder and it's a perfect recipe for bleak.

I've never been in a flood or on a boat for that amount of time, but you and I have probably both experienced some ever-long nights and days, the dark and dullness making it hard to hold onto faith. We want to believe that the sun will come up tomorrow, but if after 150 days it hasn't, well . . . it's tricky to keep hoping. Forget optimism. Glass half full? No, overflowing, and not in a good way. Plus, there's God's silence. No words from God in the time span between Cain and Noah, nor for us, perhaps.

So Genesis 8:1 knocks on the closed door of our soul with hope: "But God remembered Noah and all the wild animals and livestock that were with him in the ark." God remembered. What relief. God did not forget.

The word in Hebrew that we translate as "remembered" is often used in a way that means that God remembered with an intent to act on what was being remembered. In other words, God remembered that this family and floating zoo bobbed on the waves of despair and got ready to act.

Think of all those days and nights when you've felt forgotten—by God, by people who were supposed to love you. All those epochs of time, when the rhythm of your life synced with no one's and you felt not only out of step, but off the team. The times spent closed in with loneliness or pain or fear.

Now hear the truth: You are not forgotten. You are remembered—remembered by God, who is determined to act in your life and on the situations in your life.

Imagine Noah, floating on that literally endless sea, and the relief when the rains stopped, the wind blew, the waters receded. Not forgotten! Hallelujah, his soul surely shouted.

So it is with you. Even though the rains may not stop imme-diately. Even though the waters may not have receded and God's breath has yet to blow across the floodwaters of your soul, God has not forgotten. Not forgotten you, your situation, your loved ones. Not forgotten your pain. Not forgotten your boat in the middle of the dreadful sea.

God remembers. God will act. God will make a way and help you find your way back to dry land. At just the right time. In the meantime, sing that hymn with certainty—that heaven will come down and glory will fill your soul.

TRAVELING MERCY
Dear one,
I don't forget.
Though you feel forgotten,
You are not alone
In that boat
In the middle of the sea;
I am with you.
Though the rains fall
And the waters rise,
I am sending Someone
Who walks on water
So you will never doubt
My presence again.
Watch for me.
And don't give up.

NOTE TO SELF
Water Walker here to stay. Take hold.

THE SIGN LANGUAGE OF GOD

"As long as the earth endures, seedtime and harvest, cold and
heat, summer and winter, day and night will never cease."

—GENESIS 8:22

Our daughter Ruthie and I awakened in the dark to gather gear for our girls' getaway to Minneapolis.[1] As the night lessened, I hauled an armload of supplies outside to the cavernous car trunk. Ruthie headed out the door as I returned inside for more goodies. On my second run, I opened my mouth to share my excitement about our road trip.

But no Ruthie. The trunk yawned in the morning. Her purse, backpack, and other essentials lay scattered on the driveway. She was nowhere in sight.

At twenty years old, she'd traveled across the US and Europe for work and had returned from Germany earlier that week with a heart full of memories and memory sticks full of pictures. Because of her maturity, I wasn't worried that she'd been abducted in our quiet town. Not worried for more than a split second at least.

Because then I noticed the color of dawn. The rosy red filled the sky; the water of the nearby lake blushed to match. The entire scene shouted in sign language, "Glory." Could

Eden have been more glorious? Birds gave voice to the silent chorus as they swooped from their berths, chattering and tittering like town gossips at the flagrant display.

Of course. Ruthie ran down to the shoreline to shoot pictures, to capture this homecoming banner, this reminder of God's active presence in a world gone crazy and in her own uncertain world. Her shots of the beauty that rolled from the heavens and right up to our doorstep still grace picture frames in our home, telling the story of the Creator who created an entire world to fill it with people God loves.

Beauty. It spoke to her heart that morning, called out to her to watch, to participate. To remember and to trust the amazing Artist with her own future.

Just think: God unfurls that beauty every single day, while people hit snooze, sleepwalk through their waking moments, or are asleep to God's presence in the world around them. Though we might not notice, God doesn't stop the witness. Such extravagance seems almost wasteful to our scrimping souls with our tightwad energy and our galloping runaway fears.

Some days I move through the hours like a zombie, begging God to show up, to speak to me. Or I get lost in my long list of regrets, mired in the toll they exact on others. I don't realize that the beauty around me bears both God's signature and stamp of authority. As one friend puts it, "If the sun rises tomorrow, today's problems were not a calamity."

John Calvin said, "There is not one blade of grass, there is no color in this world that is not intended to make us rejoice." So no more of this "You snooze, you lose" life. Today, while anxieties about our economy and overwhelming work lists clink and clatter around inside me like a marble in a blender, I decide to trust the God of such beauty. To let the beauty, like Ruthie's pictures, lead me rejoicing to the One who created that surprising glory. To let God's creative message calm and restore my heart and my faith, to fling me rejoicing into my day.

Like the birds at dawn.

TRAVELING MERCY
Dear one,
You can trust me;
Will I not do right?
Look at the beauty around you
And know that I am that Author
Of all things,
Including you
And your life
And your future.
The sun rose both inside
And outside Eden.
And today,
And tomorrow
It will too,
Or you'll be with me in heaven.
Either way
You win,
And so do I.

NOTE TO SELF
Allow beauty to restore my perspective.

NOTE
1. A version of this devotion was printed as: Jane Rubietta, "The Sign Language of God," *indeed* Magazine, September/October 2011, 18–19.

NIGHT WATCH

"As long as the earth endures . . . day and night will never cease."
—GENESIS 8:22

The light creeps over the horizon as I leave the building. Though clouds cover the vault overhead, the soft whiteness beginning to glow tells me that the last shreds of darkness will soon lose the battle for domination.

In the just-built apartment complex where my family is spending the holidays, floodlights shine brightly all night long, the security-enhancing glare broadcasting a warning to anything that comes alive or prowls in the dark. But even with the dawn, the area remains silent. The holidays have silenced the usual running engines and the exhaling tail pipes. People sleep in, their windows dark. A rogue but determined southern snowfall frosted the cars with an inch of thick wet lace, and in this cocoon I wait and listen.

The last of the nocturnal creatures to put away their night vigil surprise me. Behind these buildings stands a copse of trees, a line of protest against the advancement of what we optimistically call civilization. The trees are silhouettes in the bareness of winter, and stand in sharp relief against the brightening sky.

In the quiet, a hoot owl calls, its voice haunting, mournful, and hollow. Another answers. I pad through the parking lot like a forest creature on muted feet, listening, looking. Then, against the whitening, I spot dark ovals perched on top of high branches. The owls speak again. They call to one another. They warn of dawn's approach. They call to the receding night.

And then they disappear from sight, creatures of the dark, snugging into their roost, their wings battened down against their soft warming feathers. These night announcers go off-air, in protest against the predator-filled day.

Quiet fills the sky once again. The whiteness brightens, and the engines of the daylight start once again.

My walk continues in the crisp morning air. Though I keep moving, the hush of the dawn and the hoot of those owls settled me deeply on the inside. The quiet doesn't leave my soul. This white-skied morning respite fills me, as does the transition from night to day, from darkness to light. The simple routine of closing the blinds on the night, of opening the curtains on a new start, and of noticing the kindness of both, reassures me.

Life is not either/or: either light or dark, your choice. It's not a claim-your-own-ending situation. Life is dark, life is light, and we stand in both, like and unlike the owls hooting through the night. We are watchers on the walls of our lives, perched and waiting. We watch and call through the night, and wait for the light. And though the darkness is certain, so is the dawn. God promised.

TRAVELING MERCY
Dear one,
The watch that ends the night
Begins the day,
And so it is
And shall be forever
Until I return
And night disappears
And we live together in endless
Sunlight.
Until then,
Watch for me.
Call one another through the long night.
Wait.
The light is coming.

NOTE TO SELF
Call someone in the dark. Their dark, or yours.

WILD REMOVAL

"The fear and dread of you will fall on all the beasts of
the earth, and on all the birds in the sky, on every creature
that moves along the ground, and on all the fish
in the sea; they are given into your hands."

—GENESIS 9:2

On a jog up a steep hill, my husband reached the top and
slowed, panting. Rising high over his head, a dark furry form
towered, not twenty feet away. A bear. A big bear. The stuff of
kids' best and worst adventures and dreams and nightmares.
Rich backed up, slowly, then raced down the hill when the
bear was out of sight.

In the Upper Peninsula of Michigan, bears aren't exactly
rare, but they aren't playmates. We don't seek out bears, and
we hope they don't search us out, or our cars or cabins or
children. We call them wild animals for a reason.

So don't you wonder how all those animals stood in line,
in groups of twos or sevens, waiting to board the ark, like
children holding hands to cross the street (see Gen. 6:20;
7:2–3)? That sort of docility isn't normal for wild animals.
Hyenas cracking jokes with the kittens? The Labrador
retriever and the duckling wrestling? Lions switching their
tails and affectionately nuzzling the zebras? This never made
sense to me, with the world we've inherited. Intraspecies

friendly behavior is the stuff of viral hits on the Internet, not everyday life. "Watch tiger adopt baby puppy." "Bear and fox tumble in play." These aren't friends. These are food.

But when God told Noah in Genesis 9:2–3 that all the animals, birds, and water creatures would now be afraid of humans, my little child heart sits up and listens. Once, long ago, animals were *not* afraid of us or each other. The white horned owl would've landed on my shoulder and hooted a love song into my ear. A bear hug wasn't a stranglehold en route to the next meal, but rather a warm and safe place.

After the flood, the new world order included breaking down relationships between humans and all other living beings above, on, or below the earth. The fear we see today is post-flood fallout. "Everything that lives and moves about will be food for you," God said (Gen. 9:3). Once, just the plants. Now, everything. So animals, birds, and fish literally run for their lives when they see us coming (or when they run for ours). The loss of the innocent simplicity of relationships mutes me with wordless sorrow.

Once we were all friends. Now we — and they — are foe. Fear and dread.

Not for forever though. One day the wolf will live with the lamb. The leopard will be crib mates with the goat; the cow and the bear will share a trough and their babies nap together. Lions will eat straw like the ox rather than eat the ox, and babies will play near vipers' dens. "They will neither harm nor destroy on all my holy mountain," God says (Isa. 11:9).

One day, one glorious day, all fear will disappear and "the earth will be filled with the knowledge of the LORD" (Isa. 11:9).

Neither harm nor destroy. Fear disappears, replaced with knowledge of God, replaced by peace. It sounds like heaven.

Maybe we can get started now.

TRAVELING MERCY
Dear one,
Know me,
Know peace,
Know friendship,
Know hope.
Know no more fear.
Start now.
Better days,
Coming soon.

NOTE TO SELF
Work on bear hugs.

FEBRUARY 18

FOOTPRINTS

"I will remember my covenant between me and you
and all living creatures of every kind."

—Genesis 9:15

I missed the fox.[1] Even after planting myself in front of the window, working, writing, praying, and reading. Even after moving my chair so I could see the fox's haunts—the remnants of the vegetable garden where it found delectable little voles, the oak trees with rambunctious squirrels, even the pole that held up the dilapidated bird house. Engrossed in my readings, I missed the fox's foray through our yard.

But it visited, leaving footprints in the snow, the unmistakable sign of its presence and persistence in providing for its adorable babies we sometimes saw frolicking nearby.

Days have passed without a sighting, but those footprints thrill me—the fox is alive. It wasn't a victim on the highway bordering our yard. It didn't fall through the ice on the lake. That reassures this mother heart, this heart that yearns for God's creation to be safe, to be provided for and not preyed upon.

The snow gives it away. And isn't that the only way we see footsteps, through the evidence left after they've been laid down? The fox's footprints, like so much of nature, remind me.

We see the wind because of its effect on us — the coolness on our skin, the chill on faces sweating from labor, the rustle of leaves and the clacking of branches, the howling against the doors and windows of our lives.

Isn't it so with God? Isn't this how we see and recognize God's presence and movement, stealthy and invisible to our distracted eye? "No one can see God," but we see proof of God's company. The bustling trees. Footprints in the snow. We witness creation, so reminiscent of Eden, and the combinations of circumstances so imaginative that they can only be God's tracks in the inclement weather of our lives.

If not for the fresh, clean, quiet snow, I wouldn't know of the fox's visit. While I wish I'd seen its little black legs, pointy nose, and the thick winter fur ending in that soft, bushy tail, those footprints offer lovely proof of its presence.

Now quiet, I watch. I consider the issues weighting my soul like heavy, wet packing snow on fragile branches: children's needs, ministry conundrums, looming deadlines, more work than we can handle alone, health issues for people I love, a fixer-upper house begging for intervention. I consider these, and then look again at the footprints in the snow. Just because I didn't see the fox can't eradicate the fact of its visit.

Just because we can't see God, though troubles be unceasing, we can search the landscape. We can train ourselves to notice, still ourselves so we see the signs. And though snow is often problematic, footprints are seen best in inclement weather, those snowy, muddy, powerless places of our lives.

My joy swells because I witness the proof of God's presence in my life as well. A letter from a woman in New York, perfectly timed to reassure me of God's calling. The surprise visit from a friend, bearing dinner in her arms and balloons to celebrate a happy occasion, reminds me that I am not alone — my Savior lives! And he ever lives to care for me and to carry me into God's glorious presence. God has not forgotten the promise between heaven and us and all living creatures.

I see, and it is good. I can trust one more day, parked at this window overlooking the world, and God's footprints in it.

TRAVELING MERCY
Dear one,
Just watch for my presence
Past and present,
And trust that for the future —
Because you can trust me;
I am the faithful God.
Always.
We have an everlasting covenant.
A forever yes.
Yes?

NOTE TO SELF
Recognize God; win over worry.

NOTE
1. Portions of this devotion appeared as: Jane Rubietta, "Footprints," *indeed* Magazine, January/February 2013, 6–7.

THE LONG ARCH

"Whenever the rainbow appears in the clouds,
I will see it and remember the everlasting covenant
between God and all living creatures."

—GENESIS 9:16

Off the boat after 370 days, overwhelmed with ship-craziness and overcome by the new solid ground, the Edenic restart under their feet, Noah and his family sacrificed a massive burnt offering of every type of clean animal and bird. God breathed deeply of the rich aroma. And the Maker and re-Maker of heaven and earth pledged to Noah, "I will remember my covenant between me and you and all living creatures of every kind. Never again will the waters become a flood to destroy all life" (Gen. 9:15).

Scripture uses the word *covenant* 332 times. The first covenant, to Noah and his family and the world, was signed by a rainbow. The archway reminded God, Noah, the world, and us that God would not destroy in this way, ever again.

The next covenant is a land covenant with Abraham, his barren wife, and their unborn family. Talk about hope. Since then, God made covenants to keep with mankind, for human beings to keep with God, and for people to keep with one another. Covenants of circumcision, sacrifice, and law.

We watch the progress of these covenants, knowing that we can keep none of them ourselves, knowing our own feebleness, our inadequacies. Knowing that, given the choice between life and death, we will far too often choose death. How many times have we broken covenant with our God? Daily, perhaps? I am Eve in Eden, again and again. See, take, eat.

And how many times has God broken covenant with us? Rhetorical question. Answer: none.

So the rainbow covenant led to a land covenant with Abraham that led to a circumcision (relationship) covenant that led to the ark of the covenant that led to the fulfillment of the covenant by the Son of the covenant.

Wait. What?

We hurtle along after Noah, Abraham, Moses, the Israelites, and the prophets, and skid to a halt at Malachi, to whom God said, "'The LORD you are seeking will come to his temple; the messenger of the covenant, whom you desire, will come,' says the LORD Almighty" (Mal. 3:1).

And God came to earth, wrapped in flesh and blood, God with us. That Emmanuel-God would stand with friends at the Passover feast, raise a cup of wine, offer thanks, give it to them, and say, "Drink from it, all of you. This is my blood of the covenant, which is poured out for many for the forgiveness of sins" (Matt. 26:27–28).

Forgiveness of sins? The total wrap-up, from first sin to the first murder to the plunge into evil, we find in the covenant of the One who fulfills both sides of the agreement.

"You have come to God . . . to Jesus the mediator of a new covenant, and to the sprinkled blood that speaks a better word than the blood of Abel" (Heb. 12:23–24). Abel who unwillingly died; Christ, who willingly shed his blood, sealing the new covenant.

The good news just doesn't stop. God "has made us competent as ministers of a new covenant" (2 Cor. 3:6), the covenant of the Spirit. God's breath in us, enabling us to keep, and share, the covenant with others.

And if that's not enough, hear this, weary, covenant-breaking, relationship-longing soul: "May the God of peace, who through the blood of the eternal covenant brought back from the dead our Lord Jesus, that great Shepherd of the sheep, equip you with everything good for doing his will" (Heb. 13:20–21).

Eternal covenant? Fully equipped to do God's will? Well. Noah must be tickled. That's some rainbow effect.

TRAVELING MERCY

Dear one,
The rainbow reaches
From Noah through Jesus
To you,
And confirms
My love for you,
My provision for you,
My making a way
For you.
From Eden until today
I've prepared the way.
Now you will prepare the way
For others.
Breathe in my Spirit
Fully equipped
For doing my will.
You're welcome.

NOTE TO SELF

Fully equipped. What's next?

TRAUMA REACTION

Noah, a man of the soil, proceeded to plant a vineyard.

—GENESIS 9:20

Once those grapevines bore fruit, Noah cooked up a batch of wine and tippled a bit too much, until he toppled over. *Tsk tsk*, we say. Not OK. An embarrassing display after a difficult story to swallow in the first place.

But, perhaps, understandable. Maybe all the trauma was too much for him—imagine hearing screams of terror outside the walls of the ark. Being on a ship and seeing the bloated bodies of all those people who refused the saving grace of that ridiculous ark they'd loved to lampoon floating past. How could Noah not feel some sense of post-traumatic stress disorder? How could he not feel the blunt bludgeoning ax of tragedy, the loss of life?

So many people who survive trauma of any sort resort to mind-numbing tactics—anything to not feel the pain, to not see the images that press against their eyelids with every blink. Maybe they engage in high-risk activity, something that throws their lives into jeopardy (and perhaps, if they lose their bet with risk, they will be like the ones who didn't make it). The temporary buzz kills the guilt and dulls the pain, at least until the buzz dies.

Maybe they become control freaks, managing their own little corner of the world with an iron fist and pummeling obstacles (people included) into submission. Or perhaps they play Russian roulette, either literally or with the manic high of gamblers throwing all their chips on one tiny wedge of a wheel. Maybe they have wee little—or big—issues with anger or depression.

Noah's heroics likely dimmed in his own mind, probably as soon as he pulled up the walkway in the pounding rain before leaving the dock. He'd listened to God, when no one else in the world seemed to have ears to hear or the heart to respond. He'd gone against popular opinion, building an ark that people only mocked.

Who would blame Noah for trudging with shaking legs off that rocking boat, perched on the precipice of a new-again world, and when the grapes ripened at last, for plucking and stomping a few and indulging in some desperate wine?

A lot of people would begrudge him that indulgence—or rather, that escape. Godly people don't do that. People who are healthy don't do that. How dare Noah ruin our image of him!

But more than that, we don't want to be disappointed with our heroes because we want someone who will carry the image forward. And if we can be angry with their humanity, then we don't have to focus on our own grape-smashing, wine-drinking diversions in whatever manifestation.

The more important response, I guess, is for us to under-stand that people's behavior makes psychological sense if we know the context and their story. Recognizing that wounds often lead to off-center, unhealthy reactions moves us away from self-righteousness and much closer toward mercy.

And really, that ship, that gigantic boat, hammered into place in the middle of dry land, displayed mercy. Hope. Future.

That's the message to listen to, and that's the one to give. To ourselves in our painful reactions, and to others in theirs. Wouldn't Noah be grateful?

TRAVELING MERCY

Dear one,
Mercy wins.
Consider the pain,
Consider the context,
Consider the humanity.
And know this:
My love doesn't change,
Nor my hope
For you
In all your Noah moments
And days and weeks and years.
Not for a minute
Will I give up on you.
So please
Receive the gift of mercy
So you can share it
Freely.

NOTE TO SELF

Check mercy levels.

FINDING YOUR WAY THROUGH PAIN

A cheerful heart is good medicine, but a
crushed spirit dries up the bones.

—PROVERBS 17:22

From Adam and Eve through Noah, our first families found their way without benefit of modern-day counsel. They had no growth groups, life coaches, or grief and bereavement specialists. They lacked earthly guidance to help them transition from pain to purpose.

An acronym helps us move through depression, but with far broader applications for general recovery. It's simple, but maybe grief recovery is at first basic. In addition to giving ourselves permission to weep, to actually feel the pain of loss, we can try SELF: sleep, exercise, laughter, food.

Sleep. Sleep isn't overrated—it's essential to healing the mind, body, and soul. Though depression may turn life to lethargy, real rest restores. Figure out how much sleep is healing (day and night in bed would be overdoing it—see the next tool) and give yourself permission to sleep. Reduce or eliminate activities and foods that interfere with sleep, and let go of all shoulds: shouldn't be tired, shouldn't be down, shouldn't be crabby. PPD, PTSD, grief, and stress leave us tired, down,

touchy, even angry. Accept that and employ sleep as an antidote. There's no shame in needing sleep as a recovery tool.
Since the world's creation, sleep is a God-endorsed and
recommended activity and therapy.

Exercise. Depression steals our energy and pulls the plug on
any adrenalin we might naturally experience. Movement combats and counteracts loss of energy, a major symptom of depression. Losing muscle tone and endurance due to inactivity means
that activity becomes tiring. It's a downhill somersault. Find an
exercise partner who understands grief and loss, then be deliberate about movement. The endorphin load alone is worth it, but
the enhanced energy and strength will help reset your normal.

Laughter. Nothing seems funny in the darkness of depression.
Imagine when Adam and Eve discovered laughter—peals of
chiming joy like a carillon ringing out in that first garden.
Grief makes you wonder if you will ever smile again, let alone
laugh. But don't believe the lie that says laughter cheapens
grief or the value of the person (or dream or health or other
precious thing) you've lost. Instead, laughter reminds us that
we are still alive. Like exercise, it releases healing endorphins,
decreases stress hormones, and improves circulation. A natural
painkiller, laughter boosts immune function, lowers fears,
improves perspective, and enhances relationships. Find places
to laugh. You'll join the crowd of people throughout the ages,
who say, "I feel better. Whew, I needed that."

Food. Including such a basic requirement seems silly. We
need food to stay alive. But food is a barometer of our soul
state, and making healthy and healing choices with food isn't
necessarily natural in the grips of depression, grief, and other

trauma. We want feel-good food (high calorie, high fat, sweet, salty—pampering food without super nutritional benefit) or drinks (soda, alcohol, and caffeine all provide a temporary boost and then a steep drop). Or we punish ourselves by not eating, or even bury our grief by overeating. Alongside medical and psychological care, one emergency room immediately treated suicidal patients to a steak. Perhaps because the high protein content coupled with taste helped both brain and psyche. So make a meal plan, featuring plates full of colorful whole foods, and watch your energy and hope rise.

SELF It isn't selfish to take care of yourself. Healing is a gift you give yourself, yes. But it is also a gift you give the world.

TRAVELING MERCY
Dear one,
Common sense in difficult places
Isn't all that common,
But don't be afraid
To take care of yourself.
I heartily endorse your health
And your healing journey.
You'll find your way
As you recognize your pain,
And you'll be surprised
At how purposeful
Healing becomes.
It's a gift.
From me to you.
Yours to yourself.
Ours to the world.

NOTE TO SELF
Self-care isn't selfish.

FEBRUARY 22

THE WRONG TABLE

Noah woke from his wine and found out what
his youngest son had done to him.

—Genesis 9:24

Noah got off the ark, tended his vineyard, and rejoiced in the new life. The grapes plumped up so nicely and made such a delightful wine. And then that little uncovering episode, and Noah's cursing and blessing for his sons. An all-new world, and right away, this heartbreak.

Isn't this how it works for us, too? We just about get a new start on life or faith or relationship, and perhaps actually wake up one day and have a dynamic and living experience of the life God invited us into. Then the little bubble of perfection pops and splatters, and we're left with the reality of brokenness. That ugly death chime that started with a single bite in Eden starts rolling around between our ears: "You will die, you will die, you will die."

Only this isn't the voice of God. It's the voice of the Enemy of our souls, the one who doesn't want us to live life, abundantly or at all, and doesn't want us to live the eternal life God is giving us in Christ minute by minute of every single day until we get to heaven.

We must identify that voice. This happens, for instance, when we stop to ask, "Where am I eating of the knowledge of evil? Where am I intimately acquainted with death? What are my death choices, this very moment of this particular day?"

Sometimes, a death choice is about choosing to believe a lie whispered to us: "Take that comment personally, very personally. It means that you are not loved." We chomp with gusto and then have seconds.

Or, "Hold on to that anger, child. You deserve better. Stay angry." Believing that anger vindicates us, we nurture it like small bits of burning tinder and kindling until it becomes a blaze inside. Go ahead, carry that grudge, exhaust yourself with the weight of bitterness. Death, not life.

Any time we separate ourselves from relationship, any time we believe that relationships are expendable, we choose death. Any time we grumble or complain, we choose death. The Hebrew term is *lashon hara*, meaning "malicious tongue," but it also refers to saying something that is true but negative, unnecessary, and damaging. Find some friends who are not afraid to stop you in the middle of a harangue with *lashon hara*.

We can push away from the funeral table. We can choose to move away from those lethal drumbeats, from the dinner date with death. Not by ignoring the anger, or the unloving comment, or the creeping root of bitterness or disappointment. Notice it, but then decide what is true. Those words and feelings lead to life only if we choose to examine them and take them to God, then take positive and decisive action. Otherwise, hear the bell toll.

Don't let the Enemy yank your chain and start the death chimes. Choose life. And when you eat from the wrong table, push away and start over. Remember, it's not a dinner bell. It's a death chime.

TRAVELING MERCY
Dear one,
Get to know me.
Learn my voice.
You will learn to distinguish
Me from all the other voices
And noises in the world.
Get to know your own voice,
To recognize what your heart
Really cries out for
And what it is saying.
Shove away from the table
Of bitterness, shame, regret, and anger
And pull up a chair
At my banquet.
You have a standing invitation
To dinner.

NOTE TO SELF
At which table am I eating?

A CAPPELLA JOURNEY

These are the clans of Noah's sons. . . . From these the
nations spread out over the earth after the flood.

—GENESIS 10:32

Genesis 10 is often titled with the header, "Table of
Nations," since it lists Noah's people, dispersed across the
continent.[1] Sometimes, some of those descendants find their
way to our way station.

Sixteen college students waited outside the train station.
They hugged sleeping bags and pillows. Backpacks leaned
against their legs. When Rich and I pulled into the lot in our
separate cars, the kids released a collective lion-like roar, a
massive cheer of greeting and exuberance. I couldn't stop
smiling. When I climbed out of the car, I jumped up and down
with my arms above my head, like a call and response. Our
six-foot-five-inch son, part of the a cappella singing group,
picked me up in a hug and swung me around and around, my
feet flying out like a child's, both of us laughing.

So full of life, so compatible with each other. So polite—
their mothers would be pleased and proud. They thanked us
a hundred times each, ate twenty brats and forty burgers and
a bunch of hot dogs. Strawberries and s'mores and soda pop

and chips and potato salad and baked beans and brownies and angel food cake. They laughed, held an awards ceremony, played capture the flag, and built a bonfire.

It was a weekend escape in our humble home. We couldn't have enjoyed it more, all sixteen of them piled into the family room on blankets and sleeping bags. Sixteen pairs of shoes and sandals and boots coupled off at the door to the house. Rich and I washed and dried round after round of dishes and silverware—multiply times sixteen and it's a lot of dishes—and flipped pancakes, scrambled four dozen eggs, and stuffed leftover brats and hot dogs into leftover buns for one last morsel of home before college took precedence.

The clock raced when we wanted it to drag, and the train schedule demanded a return. We crowded them all into our vehicles and carpooled back to the station.

A few minutes early, we stood around the parking lot, them hugging their pillows and sleeping bags, their backpacks leaning against their legs. They hummed the start of a song, with two of the guys doing mouth percussion. I wanted to video them to hold on to the memory but settled on being fully present.

The train whistled only a few measures into the song. My heart leaped to my throat. Mother and good-bye should not be in the same parking lot together.

They hugged us on the way by, and we got to love on them and bless them, their week, their finals, and their summers. They piled onto the train while we stood waving, the sun shimmering bright.

And as we pulled away from the empty station in our empty cars, I held back tears and tried to swallow my heart back down. Into the empty, echoing house through separate doors because of the separate cars, and still the tears heavy on my chest. I waited with them, those tears, trying to name them, and replayed the fifteen-hour period in my mind, from first cheer to final wave.

My tears were about more than missing the students in our back-to-empty nest. Every time we open our arms and heart and home to love others, we become a way station for God. We're the ark, and the nations have come for a visit. We offer cold water—or soda or steaming coffee—in Jesus' name and he says, "You did this for me." These children from other homes and other faiths and perhaps no faiths—for a brief moment, we intersect and bless them with the love of heaven, with all the hugs they'll accept. Someday, may they'll welcome that love into their hearts. And then won't that table of nations be filled?

Hastening that day, we keep on loving. And filling our fridge. In Jesus' name.

TRAVELING MERCY
Dear one,
Open your arms,
Your home,
Your heart,
And your fridge
In my name.
And won't people
Notice me?
With full stomachs and full hearts
We will rejoice together.
Do you hear the cheer,
The call and response?
Heaven's coming through,
Right on time.

NOTE TO SELF
Fill self and fridge. Open. Share.

NOTE
1. A version of this devotion was printed as: Jane Rubietta, "A Cappella Journey," *indeed* Magazine, March/April 2012, 4–5.

FEBRUARY 24

MAKING A NAME

"Come, let us build ourselves a city, with a tower that reaches
to the heavens, so that we may make a name for ourselves."

—GENESIS 11:4

Who doesn't want to be remembered? At least, remembered
with fondness, for their positive actions and contributions.
With love, appreciation, delight, even laughter. The desire to be
remembered positively tomorrow, gives purpose to our todays.
The saddest funerals my husband ever leads are those where
people remember no stories, have nothing to say about the
departed, now lying icy cold in the casket at the front of the
room. Or those funerals where only a few sober-faced and
silent people show up. The best ones? Once a man brought
his guitar and sang his closest friend's favorite song to a
delighted crowd. The best funerals include tales of significance
and impact, funny stories, laughter. And tears.

Who doesn't want to be remembered? To be remembered
is to have mattered to the world.

The people of Babel were no different. Behind their
words, "Let us make a name for ourselves," they wanted to
be remembered. They wanted to live on in people's hearts and
memories. They accomplished this by having large families,

and, they hoped, through certain post-mortem traditions: Visit the deceased's grave often, say the name frequently, have memorial meals at the tombstones, keep the name and thus the memory alive. This would help the dead in the afterlife and create continuity between the living and the dead, somehow securing the dead's vitality.

The possibility of not being remembered is terrifying. It suggests that life here is in vain, that we've never found our way, never overcome our pain, never figured out our purpose. We want to be remembered, because it tells us that we matter. Our presence makes a difference.

For the Babel builders, being remembered could also be achieved by big adventures, or by awesome accomplishments. Building that city and the tower that reached to the highest heavens constituted both adventure and accomplishment. All who passed by could look up, shade their eyes, and say, "Obal built that. Wow! Obal was amazing. Remember Obal? And remember how he baked those bricks? What a guy." A general remembering discussion would ensue. Thus, dead Obal could enjoy his afterlife just a little bit more.

So the people built a city and a tower — a big one. A tower they hoped would become a type of entryway for God to come down and hang around for a bit, pay a little visit.

Well, that sure worked. God noticed and grew concerned about the people's intent. Reach heaven by their building projects? Try to draw close to God by work ethic and production?

And then the worst possible thing happened. Or the best. Making a name their way required continuity, community, and a whole lot of human effort. So God scattered the people, confused their language, and sent them on a journey that would ultimately entail one special group of these people being called by God's name—the name that is higher than any other name. The people of God. The people who follow after God because God is good and merciful. Faithful. Loving without end. Forgiving. The God who does not forget us.

To be called by this God's name does more than ensure we're remembered. It ensures our todays and our tomorrows. Our forevers. This calling helps us lead others to the name that is higher than any other name.

The scattering and confusion of languages wasn't the worst thing. Because it led to the very best thing, ever.

TRAVELING MERCY

Dear one,
Making a name for yourself
Really is a way of saying
You don't need my name.
So let's start over.
I remember you,
I will never forget you,
And I will give you my name.
You will be my people,
And I will be your God.
Then all you do on this earth
Draws people to my name
And to their own certain future with me.
Deal?

NOTE TO SELF

Make God's name famous.

NEW ROUTES

"Otherwise we will be scattered over the
face of the whole earth."

—Genesis 11:4

How did Adam and Eve find their way after leaving Eden? How about Cain, running around with that mark on his head? Noah, fresh off the boat and no landmarks left? And then the great scattering, all the people dispersed throughout the continent after the Babel debacle?

Probably they found their way like the rest of us in new places and new situations—with a lot of wrong turns, detours, backups, and potholed roads.

As I drove down a main artery in our new town, absolutely nothing struck me as familiar. Nothing. "I do not live here," I thought, and then I said it aloud. "I don't live here." I passed a sign for a street called Normal, and I wondered who would dare to live there. Not I. (Today I saw a street named Elk. That, too, is likely a misnomer. How long since elk lived in the Chicago suburbs?)

"I don't live here." Didn't Adam and Eve think the same thing as they looked behind them at the angel swinging a sword of fire, barring reentry to the only home they'd ever known? As they looked ahead and wandered about in their ransomed clothing? Did they miss the warmth of God's presence, the living sense of God with them? Sometimes you just need someone to talk you through the route. Or even better, to walk with you through it.

Just about every time I race off on weekly errands, I phone my parents on my cell. It feels a little juvenile, and I'm not sure of the dynamics behind my need to call them while I stop at the bank, the grocery, the gas station, or the post office. I tell myself that it is convenient to call them when I am not in the presence of my office piles or the people in my life. But the real reason, perhaps, is larger than that.

Calling my parents means calling the people I equate with home, continuity, and familiarity. Even though they, too, have moved (the same weekend we did, except three hundred miles away from us) and their now-home is not the home I grew up in. Still, phoning them feels like home.

And just about every time I call them, I end up lost. "Oops, should've turned there," I say. "Whoa, this is not the right street. Remind me not to take this shortcut again. It's the long way home."

And sometimes I just ask, "Where do I live, again?"

Of course they don't know. They can't help me figure out where I'm going or how to get there, but even so, they companion me along the way.

In spite of the detours and potholed roads, the wrong turns and the missed turns, I eventually find my way home, although sometimes I still forget we live on a one-way street. And along the way, I'm figuring out my way, finding the path, recognizing street signs and intersections automatically. Finding our way takes time.

The secret, as Adam and Eve learned, and as the Babel people found, was to not be alone en route. Together, we will find home.

TRAVELING MERCY
Dear one,
The route isn't always clear—
The signs can be unfamiliar.
The landmarks may be new or nonexistent.
Familiar takes time.
Home takes time.
And it can be a lonely route.
Find a friend.
Make a call.
You can always call me;
I'm always waiting up
For the phone to ring
And hoping it will be you
On the other end.

NOTE TO SELF
Journey together, not alone.

THE POSSIBLE IMPOSSIBLE

"Nothing they plan to do will be impossible for them."

—GENESIS 11:6

At creation, the entire world sang harmony. Creatures didn't eat one another; they all ate plants. No one even fought until outside Eden. But the communication mess-up began with the serpent's lies, and Adam followed suit. When God called to him, "Where are you?" Adam didn't answer the question straight on, by revealing his hiding place. Rather, he responded to the *where* question with a *why* and *what* answer. "I heard you . . . I was afraid . . . I was naked; I hid."

Adam initiated this verbal cover-up, and we've had a hard time communicating ever since. Even in our own language, we have difficulty saying what we mean and meaning what we say, without saying it in a mean way. And having another hear us and receive our words with our meaning still intact.

But when we get it together, watch out. There's no end to the power of good communication well sent and well received. The sky's the limit regarding possible achievement.

Generations after Adam and Eve, the "whole world had one language and a common speech" (Gen. 11:1). The people baked bricks and slathered bitumen enthusiastically, building a city with a tower to reach to heaven. God eyed the successful work at Babel. Without the best of motives, unity of language would lead to dangerous power, to mutiny and chaos. "Come," God said, "let us go down and confuse their language so they will not understand each other" (11:7).

God did, they didn't, and the building project halted because no one could send or follow instructions or offer encouragement. From there, "the LORD scattered them over the face of the whole earth" (11:9).

The power of communication and cooperation is a basic principle for success in business, in relationships, and in life. Just before scrambling the language, God said, "If as one people speaking the same language they have begun to do this, then nothing they plan to do will be impossible for them" (11:6). Unity can accomplish great good, or great evil.

God dispersed the people across the face of the earth, then narrowed the focus on Shem's family line. From his descendants, Abraham would be born. Abraham's great-great grandson would call for unity among his followers. The Messiah echoed Genesis 11:6, saying, "If two of you on earth agree about anything they ask for, it will be done for them by my Father in heaven. For where two or three gather in my name, there am I with them" (Matt. 18:19–20).

Jesus told us to pray in agreement, and then prayed that we would be one as he and God are one (John 17:11). No more infighting, no backstabbing, no gossip. No contests for superiority. Paul later beseeched the people to "agree with one another in what you say and that there be no divisions among you, but that you be perfectly united in mind and thought" (1 Cor. 1:10). Imagine what unity among believers would say to the world! Millions of Christ-followers, living in unity and drawing others into the miracle of community.

Our unity brings praise to God. Our unity brings Christ's presence. Our unified prayers before God bring God's answers. And one day, we will unite in harmony, every tribe, nation, people, and language, to declare, "Salvation belongs to our God, who sits on the throne, and to the Lamb" (Rev. 7:9–10).

No more Babel. Rather, thousands of tongues singing our great Redeemer's praise. It's time for choir practice.

TRAVELING MERCY

Dear one,
Unity will be the sign
Of your love for me
And my presence in you
And my work through you.
A miracle!
So much to disagree about.
But find your commonality—
Christ in you,
The hope of all glory,
Christ through you,
The only hope
For this Babel-ing world.
Nothing is impossible.
Including unity.
And through unity.

NOTE TO SELF

Dispel dis-chord with harmony.

BLESSED CONFUSION

The LORD scattered them over the face of the whole earth.

—GENESIS 11:9

In one church we served, people entered the sanctuary through a doorway beneath an eight-foot-wide stained-glass window. The window, a memorial donation, bore the donor's name prominently in the corner normally reserved for the artist's name or Scripture reference.

Wanting to be remembered is human nature, and building monuments to ourselves is part of our ego-stoking to ward away our own fears of insignificance. Don't we all succumb to this at times? By keeping Noah's extended family on the move through the Babel dispersion, God made it harder for them to erect statues in their own memory or for their own glory. For many reasons, Babel was good.

Some rabbis believe Genesis 11 occurred before Shem, Ham, and Japheth parted ways in Genesis 10. Was the scattering and three-stranded division of humanity simply a judgment after Babel, or was there more?

Perhaps Babel was a course correction for us, or a fine-tuning, regarding the broader mission. The more settled we got in our last home, the more stuff we accumulated. And the easier it was to lose sight of God over the towers of belongings (an interesting word, *belongings*, speaking of significance) and towering financial responsibilities. We become silly or hoarding or shortsighted, the stronger and more planted we get. And the more planted, the more territorial; the more monuments, the more munitions needed to protect them.

How did we slide from paradise in Eden to such an unhappy, violent human family by Genesis 6:13? What didn't we already have that caused us to raise yet another club to a brother or sister, and perhaps take our neighbor's wives and daughters by force (see 6:5)?

In the United States, we settled such large tracts of cotton-growing land that it became necessary to import conscripted labor to reap the land's profit. Look at Hitler's thirst for land and domination, and the resultant bloodshed and destruction. We get settled and we get greedy. And how easy then to forget God's mission.

In some ways, the original mission statement in Genesis 1:28 (and again in 9:7) is a bit uninspiring: Be fruitful and multiply. Eat, copulate, and procreate. It really doesn't call forth much from us that is more difficult or inspiring than for the rest of the animal kingdom. What happened, when our loftiest goal was eating, having sex, and acquiring resources?

We have continued to recreate chaos in the world by taking dominion of our neighbors' stuff while being unable to subdue our own wills.

In the dispersion of Babel and the table of nations, God moves people toward a higher standard, regardless of their epoch. We're expanding with "Be fruitful and multiply" as our base, and taking on a mission increasingly fitting for life outside of perfection, a more specific filling out of our purpose: "I will make your name great and *you will be a blessing*" (Gen. 12:2, emphasis added). By confusing and scattering us, God directed us toward a deeper calling through Abram, who hit the road by Genesis 11:31. He would be a sojourner all his days, and his progeny after him.

From Adam to Noah, to Shem, to Abraham. To Jesus. The angels cast a new vision of God's vision at Christ's birth, a 100 percent shift from the chaos and evil before the flood and from the terrors of the deep.

So how can we help ourselves from the destruction of our settledness? How can God save us from our own rampage to dominate each other and other nations?

We find our way as we focus on how to be a blessing. There's plenty of purpose undergirding every single step of our day. Blessing. A mighty powerful means of bearing fruit and multiplying.

TRAVELING MERCY
Dear one,
Settle into my care for you,
My name for you,
And work toward this new goal
For you.
Be fruitful, yes.
Multiply, yes.
But bear fruit through loving,
And multiply through peacekeeping.
I have blessed and will continue to bless you.
How about
Paying it forward?

NOTE TO SELF
Revisioning. Bear fruit by blessing.

A NEW MAP APP

Do not be afraid, for I am with you.

—Isaiah 43:5

Whether we are eighteen or eighty-eight, whether our whole life lies before us like a long winding road, or the bulk of our life trails behind us, a ribbon in the winds of time—whatever our stage in life, life always unfurls before us. Every single day a newborn hope, unlived, fresh, awaiting our entrance.

However this bright new moment or day unfolds, with its questions and dilemmas, its unknowns and wish-we-hadn't-knowns, we *can* know this for sure: Just as an angel guarded the way to the Tree of Life, thousands of years later a man proclaimed, "I am the way, the truth, and the life" (John 14:6). The guard has been removed, the gate opened, and a welcome mat placed at the door.

That truth has never changed, although situations and relationships have. Whatever our unknowns—a yawning chasm called the future, a graduation or job change, a bare ring finger, an empty bank account and wallet—whatever those uncertainties, we will find our way. God promised, and sent us the Way.

When we open our map app and realize the only blinking dot is where we are, that no highlights direct us, we rely on God's truth. Psalm 23:3 says that God guides us in the paths of righteousness. In our shortsighted uncertainties, we ask, "What is the way of righteousness here? How do I align myself with God, with God's priorities, in this situation, this unknown?"

With our gaze blindfolded and the terrain uncharted, God knows, and God promised to trail-blaze. "I will lead the blind by ways they have not known, along unfamiliar paths I will guide them" (Isa. 42:16).

When boulders tumble, when darkness masks us, when our souls blister and our knuckles swell from gripping our walking stick with a death-hold, we transfer our clutching hands to God's Isaiah 42:16 promise, "I will turn the darkness into light before them and make the rough places smooth." I *will*, God said. Not, I might.

When our abandonment issues roar inside our heads, when shame threatens to cancel our travel plans, we again grasp God's words, "I will not forsake them" (Isa. 42:16). I will *not*, God said. We remember that God knitted us in our mothers' wombs, calling us wonderfully made (Ps. 139:13–14).

No longer can we afford to confuse finding our way with knowing where we're going. The destination is not always the point of the journey—how we travel is critical. Who are we, en route to only God knows where? If we tread the path of righteousness, then the journey is about becoming the best self ever.

In the beginning, after all, God. And then, dust of the earth and shaped by God's hand, breathed into with heavenly life, we dance onto the picture. We are not the picture nor the focus of the picture.

But we are part of the picture, and this life is not a selfie. It was not and never will be good to be alone, not always, not in entirety. Aloneness frees us to understand our unique identity, but relationships help shape us. Finding our way includes companioning well: God's companioning us and our companioning others.

On this long and rugged trail, we learn to pace ourselves, to find our way, one day at a time. We hold tightly to God, who will never allow life or circumstances to snatch us from his hand. And we try to offer our other hand to someone needing a path through pain and into purpose.

Meanwhile, hold hands when crossing the street. And don't forget to watch for the rainbow.

TRAVELING MERCY
Dear one,
I promised my companionship.
Promised to be your guide
Faithfully at your side,
Enclosing you behind and before,
Leading the way,
Lighting your path
In the darkest night,
Always directing you home,
Home with me forever.
But don't travel alone.
Take some friends,
Grow some fruit,
And let's journey onward together.
The welcome mat
Is on the stoop.
And I'll leave the light on.
I *am* the Light.

NOTE TO SELF
Holding on. Looking forward. One step at a time.

ALL THINGS NEW

In keeping with his promise we are looking forward to a
new heaven and a new earth, where righteousness dwells.

—2 Peter 3:13

The glory dulled from the just-new earth. Adam and Eve's
shame blinded all our eyes to God's brilliance in this world,
leaving us with cataracts, a veiled impression of earth. Eden,
to our shaded and jaded eyes, is unimaginable when seen
through the scrim of our sin. That first failure, then murder
right outside; before long, a world overrun with wickedness.
God, who had so delighted in creation, saw that "every inclination
of the thoughts of the human heart was only evil all the time.
The Lord regretted that he had made human beings on the
earth, and his heart was deeply troubled" (Gen. 6:5–6).

Ancient Greeks tallied seven man-made wonders around the
Mediterranean Rim. But what about the original God-made
wonders before the flood? Were they dulled, wiped out, washed
away, water-altered, mud-buried? But so many God-wonders
still exist in nature; just imagine creation's wonder.

One day—one day!—we will see the wonder restored. One
day, the angels that sang at creation will sing again at the
restoration, and we will join their unending hallelujahs.

One day, heaven and nature will sing again. One day, the rocks, fields, streams, and trees will form an orchestra— leaves clapping, earth rejoicing with harmony, descant, and dancing melody lines—and we'll join the great chorus and hymn of all creation. One day, as God's chosen ones, we will long enjoy the work of our hands (see Isa. 65:22). One day, God says, "I will create new heavens and a new earth. The former things will not be remembered, nor will they come to mind" (Isa. 65:17).

New heaven. New earth? The poison we've dumped into the ground, the sin we've spilled through bloodshed and con- tamination, through greed and toxic choices—one day, God will eradicate the impact of this and all our sin. The destruc- tion through all our building projects, the billions of pounds of concrete and blacktop covering the rich soil beneath, the wildlife we've shoved into extinction because of habitat destruction—all this gets a do-over.

And here's something equally remarkable, given what we know about the wild plummet of humane humanity since Eve's fateful and fatal bite: "If anyone is in Christ, the new creation has come: The old has gone, the new is here!" (2 Cor. 5:17). You *are* a new creation, states the emphatic Greek. Not, "You will be one day when the rest of the world is new again," but rather, "You *are*." Right now, with Christ in you, you are a new creation. We should be shaking our heads in wonder, blinking rapidly and trying to assimilate this miracle. We're one of the original wonders of the world! And we, as God's new creation, will live and love and work and worship in that new place.

The trees will dance and so will we, and we will live and twirl with God in person.

As we try to find our way out of Eden and into our future, and while we grieve the losses of relationship and of the brilliant unfaded glory of that original creation, we look ahead with hope. And we do our part right now, in our lives, in our relationships, and on this land. We, too, proclaim as choirs have for centuries, "No more let sins, and sorrows grow. Nor thorns infest the ground."[1]

We live, we love, we give, and we give back. Fruitful, multiplying, a people after God's own heart. Our lives shaped by God's love as we love God and love others. The highest purpose of all.

TRAVELING MERCY
Dear one,
Join the unending chorus,
Skies and trees,
Clouds and leaves,
All clapping their hands
And rejoicing.
I am doing a new thing
Right now,
This very day.
Do you perceive it?
One day all you see
Will pass away
And the new will come.
Meanwhile,
You are a new
Creation right now.
Live into it,
Live into *you*,
As you find your way
Every single day
To me.
And we will make a difference
In this old world
Until it, too,
Is new again.

NOTE TO SELF
Replace the old me with the new *we*.

NOTE
1. "Joy to the World," Isaac Watts, 1719, public domain.

A TRANSITIONING WORD

Her purple plastic bags were frayed, the fibers from the cheap material stuck out from the edges like strings on celery sticks. She waited on the sidewalk when I dislodged myself down the narrow bus steps. "Snacks, pain reliever, soda pop, crackers, toothbrush, toothpaste? Anything you need to make your ride easier." Her rich voice carried over the humming silence of travel fatigue and the waiting tension of new passengers.

She crossed the street three days later, while I waited for my return bus. This time she knew a queue-mate. In her travel aids, she included free advice, wisdom, ethics, and politics. Homeless for two years, she now rented an apartment. Disability pay didn't cover her rent. So fifteen dollars a day at the bus stop kept her from begging. She didn't want to turn into the scammers she'd met during her own cup-rattling.

Finding her way was no trajectory toward success, the best-dressed list, true love, or the perfect family. Pain, disappointment, and abuse tumbled into her life, like a dump truck unloading tons of gravel. But in spite of the difficulty, she got up every day. "No one asked to be born. Deal with what you've got. You are not an exception in your hard life," she said. "Unless you're the one person who did ask to be born." Now I wonder if she meant Jesus, because he did fully intend to be born. Maybe I'll ask her one day.

Meanwhile, her approach works for anyone finding their way through pain and toward purpose. As people who follow God, our journey includes its dump trucks that pour gravel and rocks and refuse onto our path. If our purpose is no higher than a pay raise or a ring on our finger, a house or a following in social media or a more fit body, we've missed our journey's point.

Our purpose must transcend our lives' logistics. The rich young man asked Jesus, "What must I do to get eternal life?" Jesus told him to obey the laws. "Done that," the man said. "Now what?"

"Sell everything you own," Jesus then explained. "Give the money away. Follow me."

The man went away crushed, for "he was holding on tight to a lot of things" (see Matt. 19:16–30 MSG).

Our purpose will permeate all the unloveliness of our lives, the not-quite-rights, the less-than places of relationship, job, church, and service. Embrace Adam's mandate, "Be fruitful and multiply," and read this through New Testament lenses. Recognize Jesus behind those words. The most important commands, he told a lawyer, were to love the Lord your God with all your heart and soul and mind and strength, and your neighbor as yourself (see Luke 10:27). Fruitful and multiplying.

With this paradigm, through this view of motive and mission, we peer through the day two schisms around us, all the places of rupture and separation that have led to hatred, bloodshed, and indelible pain. The outworkings of injustice, of skinism and favoritism in all their hues, all have a common pre-fissuring point. People, underneath their actions in this world, live and act from their brokenhearted core. From their deepest longings to be loved, to be safe, to be free. To live a life of meaning.

We are, at heart, operating with the same hope. As people finding our way, we know without question that our God transforms pain into purpose. And here, we find in our common denominator of pain the empathy required to address injustice, to work toward peace, and to invite people to the One who created the earth for the purpose of loving us.

Like those bus passengers with travel fatigue, we dislodge from our steep narrow steps and climb down to sidewalk level. "Anything you need to make your travels easier," she'd offered.

Isn't this so for us as well? We have what we need to not only travel easier, but to travel directly. We sync our agenda with Jesus' plan. We love. Love God, love our neighbor, and, day after day, learn that love heals broken hearts. Paul got it right in 1 Corinthians 12:31. It really is "the most excellent way."

See you at the bus stop.

ABOUT THE AUTHOR

Jane Rubietta's hundreds of articles about soul care and restoration have appeared in many periodicals, including *Today's Christian Woman*, *Virtue*, *Marriage Partnership*, *Just Between Us*, *Conversations Journal*, *Decision*, *Christian Reader*, *Indeed*, and *Christianity Today*. Some of her books include: *Finding Life*, *Finding the Messiah*, *Finding Your Promise*, *Finding Your Name*, *Finding Your Dream*, *Worry Less So You Can Live More*, *Quiet Places*, *Come Closer*, and *Grace Points*.

She is a dynamic, vulnerable, humorous speaker at conferences, retreats, and pulpits around the world. Jane particularly loves offering respite and soul care to people in leadership. She has worked with Christian leaders and laity in Japan, Mexico, the Philippines, Guatemala, Europe, the US, and Canada.

Jane's husband, Rich, is a pastor, award-winning music producer, and itinerant worship leader. They have three children and make their home surrounded by slightly overwhelming gardening opportunities in the Midwest.

For more information about inviting Jane Rubietta to speak at a conference, retreat, or banquet, please contact her at:

Jane@JaneRubietta.com
www.JaneRubietta.com

From Darkness to Dawn—
the Birth of Our Savior

Through artfully told daily devotions, author Jane Rubietta leads readers along a twenty-eight day journey into the heart of Advent, in search of the living Messiah. Reaching past the holiday veneer of tradition, pageantry, and glitz, she draws readers far into the spiritual depths of Christmas, where Christ can be born again into souls. This deeper approach to devotion is still accessible reading for just five to ten minutes a day.

A free group leader's guide is available at
www.wphresources.com/findingthemessiah.

Finding the Messiah
ISBN: 978-0-89827-902-3
eBook: 978-0-89827-903-0

From Eden to Gethsemane—
the Garden Restored

The life lost in Eden is found through Gethsemane. Follow author Jane Rubietta on her daily journey through the season of Lent as she traces the way that God the Son traverses with his people. Significantly, Jesus' ministry sometimes took place in garden settings: not only did he come because of what had been lost in Eden, but Jesus met with his disciples in a garden, he prayed in a garden, he was arrested violently in a garden, and he was buried in a garden tomb.

A free group leader's guide is available at
www.wphresources.com/findinglife.

Finding Life
ISBN: 978-0-89827-892-7
eBook: 978-0-89827-893-4

1.800.493.7539      wphstore.com

Finding Jesus in Every Season

Follow author Jane Rubietta on her daily journey through each season of the year to gain perspective, refresh your soul, and continue the journey. Tracing the lives of some of the Bible's greatest characters, these are transformational devotionals that encourage great depth. Walk through these stories from the Bible and experience life as these great characters did, gaining fresh faith and hope for your journey along the way.

*A free group leader's guide is available for
each devotional at www.wphresources.com.*

Finding Your Promise
(spring)
ISBN: 978-0-89827-896-5
eBook: 978-0-89827-897-2

Finding Your Name
(summer)
ISBN: 978-0-89827-898-9
eBook: 978-0-89827-899-6

Finding Your Dream
(fall)
ISBN: 978-0-89827-900-9
eBook: 978-0-89827-901-6

Finding Your Way
(winter)
ISBN: 978-0-89827-894-1
eBook: 978-0-89827-895-8